Praise for *The New Alpha Male*

"After working for success on and off the basketball court, Lance is now taking on the role of coach as he urges readers to challenge the way they approach success in their own lives—with compassion, kindness, and awareness."

NICK NURSE
head coach of the Toronto Raptors, 2019 NBA Champions

"Growing up, many men learned a certain playbook on how to live life. Most of those plays are for an outdated system that only ends up hurting people today. In *The New Alpha Male*, Lance gives us the upgraded game plan for a fulfilling life. The rules are constantly changing, and he's a great coach to learn from!"

LEWIS HOWES
author of *The Mask of Masculinity* and *New York Times* bestseller *The School of Greatness*

"Lance Allred has written such an engaging and important book for our times. In today's world we struggle with how to balance male and female energies to return to harmony and away from behaviors of domination. I was deeply touched by reading Lance's life story and how he rose above the challenges of being a male in today's world as he committed living his life to embracing his heart, passion, his authentic self, staying in his integrity, and honoring the power of perseverance. *The New Alpha Male* is a treasure!"

SANDRA INGERMAN, MA
author of twelve books, including *Walking in Light* and *The Book of Ceremony*

"*The New Alpha Male* generates workable answers and solutions to the challenges and problems men face in the complex 21st century. Lance's call for honest introspection to reach and fulfill his Principles of Perseverance begins to unravel the mystery of how men can become better partners, fathers, brothers, sons, and simply, better people. Using the game of basketball, Lance illuminates the path forward. His observations serve as beginning steps toward reconciling the male role in a progressive society swiftly bending toward shared rather than dominant leadership in our society."

LEN ELMORE
TV sportscaster, lawyer, professor at Columbia University, former NBA player, husband, and father

"In all my years covering the NBA, Lance Allred is among the great visionary athletes I've met. His story is inspirational, and his determination to turn heartache into healing has made him heroic. He is a true vessel for the best lessons of the human spirit in sports. *The New Alpha Male* is a must-read exploration into the virtues of modern manhood."

ADRIAN WOJNAROWSKI
ESPN Insider and *New York Times* bestselling author of *The Miracle of St. Anthony*

"*The New Alpha Male* affirms that perseverance is the most essential quality to success. True success is defined by a man's ability to lead and serve with a courageous heart and humble confidence in both the peaks and the valleys of life. This book is a powerful message for all men, as well as a resource for women to appreciate and value them as brave teammates and leaders."

ARIANA ROCKEFELLER
equestrian, entrepreneur, and philanthropist

"In a time when we desperately need it, Lance Allred uses basketball to speak reason to a polarized world. With his teachings on how to begin to play the game of life as a team, he brings a calming influence, and a simple approach that welcomes every walk of life."

ANDY BILLMAN
director of *Believeland*

"In an era when so many men are lost and disconnected from the true north and nourishment of a vulnerable manhood, Lance has written a book that provides a new map and compass that lead us back to the healing power of sacred masculinity. This trailblazing guide is essential medicine for our times, offering a new way to fully claim and embody all that we are as men."

ROBERT OHOTTO
intuitive strategist and bestselling author of *Transforming Fate into Destiny*

THE
NEW
ALPHA
MALE

How to Win the Game When the Rules Are Changing

LANCE
ALLRED

sounds true
BOULDER, COLORADO

Sounds True
Boulder, CO 80306

Published 2020

Cover design by Lisa Kerans
Book design by Jess Morphew

Printed in the United States of America

Library of Congress Cataloging-in-Publication Data

Names: Allred, Lance, 1981- author.
Title: The new alpha male : how to win the game when the rules are changing
    / Lance Allred.
Description: Boulder, CO : Sounds True, 2020.
Identifiers: LCCN 2019023433 (print) | LCCN 2019023434 (ebook) | ISBN
    9781683643760 (hardback) | ISBN 9781683643777 (ebook)
Subjects: LCSH: Men--Psychology. | Success.
Classification: LCC HQ1090 .A454 2020 (print) | LCC HQ1090 (ebook) | DDC
    155.3/32--dc23
LC record available at https://lccn.loc.gov/2019023433
LC ebook record available at https://lccn.loc.gov/2019023434

10 9 8 7 6 5 4 3 2 1

This book is dedicated to my son, Simon—
Sweet boy, may you always be bold.

*I believe much trouble and blood would be saved
if we opened our hearts more.*

Attributed to Chief Joseph—Hin-mah-too-yah-lat-kekt,
or "Thunder Rolling Down the Mountain"

CONTENTS

FOREWORD

The game of basketball introduced me to Lance Allred. This would make sense to anyone who knows either of us, since I have been a nationally known basketball writer and analyst for two decades and Lance is the first legally deaf player to play in the National Basketball Association. But these many years later, I have to remind myself of what first brought us together—because who I know him to be now and all that he has done since we met makes his NBA achievement, while still noteworthy, seem like a historical footnote.

When we met back in 2008, I worked for ESPN in a variety of NBA-centric roles—senior writer for its magazine, *SportsCenter* analyst, sideline reporter for both TV and radio. Lance was then a teammate of LeBron James on the Cleveland Cavaliers.

Cleveland is not exactly a popular destination in early March, but it was for Lance and me at the time. He was halfway through his first ten-day contract with the Cavaliers and had made his NBA debut in the previous game, taking the floor for the last seventeen and a half seconds in a lopsided loss to the Orlando Magic. (Still enough time for him to take and miss an eighteen-foot jumper. Fortune favors the bold.) I flew in to Cleveland to be the sideline reporter on an ESPN telecast of the Cavaliers' next game against one of their biggest rivals, the Detroit Pistons. ESPN wanted me to talk about LeBron, whereas I wanted to talk about Lance.

I should let you in on a little secret when it comes to professional sports leagues: they're big on conformity. Certainly there are some zany characters at every level—player, coach, management, owner—but how much their idiosyncrasies are tolerated is directly commensurate with how uniquely talented or powerful they are. Which is what fascinated me about Lance. As an undrafted white dude out of a mid-major school

(Weber State) who needed all four years of his college eligibility to garner any attention after getting crossways with a highly regarded coach in NBA circles, how did he crack the league? He had no relative power. And as a Montana-born, polygamist-raised, legally deaf, near seven-footer who was already twenty-seven when the Cavaliers signed him in midseason, he checked none of the boxes that generally appear on the prerequisite list for making it to the highest level of basketball: McDonald's high school All-American, NCAA tourney star, exceptional athlete, and twenty or younger being among them. Equally bad, he checked a bunch of boxes that had never appeared on the list.

As a red-headed, left-handed, first-generation American whose first words were German, I considered myself a bit of an odd box-checker myself. Even though I'm best known for covering the NBA, that's not how I define myself in my own head, as a person or a writer. Like Lance, I've never considered that where I came from might limit where I could go. Only looking back at the arc of my life do I recognize the unlikely dips and turns, such as being not just the first and only person in my family to go to college but winding up at an Ivy League school. Or, despite being a collegiate soccer player, becoming a national authority on my second love, basketball. Or writing a book with China's Yao Ming, the first foreign-born and foreign-developed player ever to be the first pick in an NBA draft, despite having no previous ties to China or basketball in Asia.

I say none of that now with any sort of conceit, although I once might have. I realize now how my life arc was not shaped by my ambition and effort, but more so by the people I connected with along the way, people that I was *able* to connect with because I dedicated my effort to connecting with them, not my ambition.

Lance has gone through the same evolution when it comes to making it to the NBA: understanding that the value received isn't in the status the achievement afforded him, but rather what he learned from the relationships built along the way that got him there.

The question remains: how does making it to the NBA provide valuable insight into making it as a man in today's world, where the definition of healthy masculinity is being revised on a daily basis?

That's easy. I've yet to see a successful player or team that wasn't able to put aside personal interpretations of masculinity to embrace one shaped by the team as a whole—escaping their personal "polygamy," as Lance describes in his popular TEDx talk. What makes Lance's perspective valuable is not that he reached the NBA but everything he overcame to get there and the perspective he attained seeing it from the inside out.

This is what I know as a fellow odd box-checker: all the aspects of Lance's life that make him "fit out rather than fit in"—to use LeBron's phrase—are not disadvantages, but rather major benefits. To paint him as a former NBA player is laughably limiting. There is value in knowing precisely what it takes to reach that elite echelon, but I'm sure the collective experience of ten years playing in Puerto Rico, Japan, Spain, Italy, Qatar, Mexico, Turkey, France, Greece, and Venezuela was far greater. Lance has seen the world from a different viewpoint, literally and figuratively—not just from being born in the largest stretch of undeveloped wilderness of the continental United States and being raised in an extreme religious sect and coping with a major handicap but by being part of basketball teams in wildly different conditions and cultures all over the world. I can't think of a better way to see through stereotypes and preconceived notions than working intimately with people from nearly a dozen different cultures.

Those who grow up on the fringes of society—or don't easily identify with a certain group or belief system or heritage and seek to connect with others in a meaningful way—have little choice but to look outside of themselves and their particular (and most likely peculiar) circumstances. Their senses are inherently heightened to see, hear, and feel what their fellow man is doing because it's the only way they're going to find common ground. Their uniqueness means that every relationship requires them to reach out and find the touchstones shared with that particular person. That's true for every relationship, but most of us find the path leveled and groomed to some extent by similarities in how we look or talk or what we do. A cat accepted by a pack of dogs knows more about what it takes to befriend a dog than any of the dogs. As I see it, Lance has been a cat in pretty much every phase of his life, searching for a way into one pack of dogs or another. He's an outlier.

Chances are anyone reading this has felt the same way, particularly if you're male. I know I have. We—men, that is—are a much more varied species than we've been led to believe. The John Wayne/Vin Diesel/Frank Castle template is proof that, for all we might think our mentality about masculinity has evolved, the most popular version is still playing the same simplistic tune on the same limited range of bells—a mentality that might play well in movies but doesn't in real life. So, what does?

Stumbling out of the Montana wilderness, like a modern day Percival, Lance Allred offers valuable tools from his experiences of extremes, extracting truths about the world at large along the way. A man intimately familiar with both dominance and vulnerability in all their forms, he has written a fearlessly introspective treatise on being a man in today's world. Lance doesn't offer a new template as much as a set of tools to create your own. And I invite you to do so. For if Lance's life is proof of anything, it's that what kind of man you are is what kind of man you choose to be.

Ric Bucher

PREGAME

Rebound

THE LIGHTS ARE SO BRIGHT. Brighter than the sun, or so it seems as I step up to the line to shoot my first free throw in the NBA in front of 16,000 people in Cleveland, Ohio. I take one dribble for rhythm and wind up to shoot like I have a hundred thousand times before, my brain and muscle memory set.

I look up to the rim with soft focus, never aiming, which was what allowed me to be a career 80 percent free-throw shooter—rare for a big man. Whenever you are in your head and not your body, you miss. Aiming the shot is overthinking and kills flow and rhythm.

"Stay in your body," I whisper to myself at the free-throw line; my first mistake as a small, insidious thought, pushes back: *Is this it? Is this the best that it gets? Why don't I feel any different?*

This thought is so sinisterly quiet that it is louder in my head than the rumble of the arena. Although I can't really hear ambient sound, I feel it, yet my internal question is louder as it asks again, *Is this it?*

I am rattled. I take my shot, and the mechanical process of muscle memory is off as my brain short-circuits. The ball launches in an awkward *push* with no backspin. I follow the ball with my eyes as it sails past the rim and hits the backboard, caroming into the hoop.

Bank.

My first point in the NBA was an unintentionally banked-in free throw off the glass. Most people thought I had done so on purpose, since I was a bank-shot expert and had even won the H-O-R-S-E Trophy with a variety of bank shots a month earlier at NBA All-Star weekend in New Orleans, Louisiana, as a D-League Star. The bank shot is a lost art. Some might call it boring, relying on the backboard to carom your ball into the hoop. To me it is beautiful, namely for its simplicity. But I never banked my free throws.

My new teammates laughed and patted me on the back, yet I wasn't laughing.

What happened at the free-throw line? Was it nerves? That was an easy explanation, but the truth is it was the voice in my head pointing out how the illusions of worldly success I had chased for so long were in fact hollow, and how unfulfilled I still felt in my heart.

Sure, my ego was happy. I was in the NBA—*bragging rights, yo.*

Yet in my heart all I felt was fear.

Fear that I wasn't enough.

Fear that this new job, my contract, my stability might be taken away from me. The same fear that so many of my teammates on the Cleveland Cavaliers were feeling as well: fear that we were expendable, fear that if we lost this job, we would have no value to the world. Depression set in.

Yes, there I was—in the NBA, a lifelong dream for so many, and I was hit with depression. Because if the NBA and those bright lights couldn't make me happy, what could?

My depression resulted in a near suicide attempt within the year, following the 2008 recession when I, like so many other players in the league, was released by the Cleveland Cavaliers due to budget concerns.

As I slowly recovered from that nervous breakdown, I had a choice:

Does the hero fall to hubris and stubbornness, unwilling to heed the lesson?

Or does the hero transcend and transform?

I chose to adapt. I chose to rebound. I chose transformation.

I changed so many things—not just my thoughts, values, how I measured success, or the stories that fueled my fears, but most importantly, I began to challenge my logic that drove said values, stories, fears. Logic that said my worth as a modern American man was contingent on external trophies.

I made that commitment in 2009.

I wrote this book a decade later.

It took me ten years of transformation—the daily grind and grueling work of internal accountability and reflection—as I traveled the world playing basketball on every continent except Antarctica to reach the point where I could write this book. I did not go live in a vegan commune to withdraw from life, leaving my responsibilities behind. Rather, I chose accountability, and faced my life head-on as I ended my basketball career, went through a divorce, and became a single father.

I chose to adapt. I chose to rebound. I chose transformation.

Transformation is perseverance. It is grit.

How did I transform?

By returning to the basics and fundamentals my great coaches taught me and looking at them from a fresh angle while relying on my core play that carried me for ten years as a professional basketball player: *the rebound.*

Because I had 80 percent hearing loss and an inability to wear hearing aids while playing basketball due to potential sweat and collision damage (having once had my hearing aid shatter in my ear canal), along with the concussion risks, I had a heavy set of challenges. Including the natural inner-ear imbalance from hearing loss, I came to the game later than most people—I first picked up a basketball at age fourteen as a way to adjust to my new life after my family escaped a Mormon fundamentalist polygamous cult. While other kids had been playing junior league basketball, I'd been preparing for the Second Coming of Jesus.

Given my inner-ear imbalance, hearing loss, and my late start, I was a bit behind. I had to adapt, learning to play differently from most other players. I had to rely on sight and touch as well as my intuition, which took some time to trust. I also had to be willing to do things nobody else wanted or needed to do, the kinds of things that aren't measured on stat sheets, like:

- » Dive onto the floor for loose balls.
- » Outrun everyone else on the court (even the smaller, speedy guards) despite my 6' 11" frame.
- » Keep my head on a swivel, sharpening my peripheral vision with a constant soft focus to see everything happening on the court simultaneously.
- » Study body language to predict who was preparing to receive the ball and who was psychologically vulnerable.
- » Communicate—sometimes way too stridently in a quiet gym where I couldn't tell how loud I was—because if I couldn't hear my teammates on defense, at least I could be the one talking.

» Choose to stand up every time I got knocked down, which was a lot since I was unable to hear my teammates call out when screens were coming my way.

» Master the art of the free throw as a big man. As they say, "Dunks for show, free throws for dough."

And of course, the rebound. While rebounding for sure is measured on the stat sheet, it is something more—it is an affair of the heart. Crafty scoring was fun, but for me, rebounding was always my favorite part of basketball. Nothing satisfied me more than the rebound, timing it just so, and snatching the missed shot out of the air in perfect rhythm while other players clawed at your arms.

You wanted it more. That was all.

It was so simple. So human.

Sure, there were some fundamentals and footwork involved with the rebound along with studying other players to figure the angle their missed shots would take, but at the end of the day it was simple: *Who wanted it more?*

The average age of an NBA rookie is twenty years old. I was twenty-seven when I joined the Cleveland Cavaliers as the first legally deaf player in NBA history. That was seven extra years of setbacks, heart-breaks, and disappointments.

What dream would you chase if you knew it would take you seven years longer than everyone else? What quiet path would you walk if you knew it would be another ten years before you share what you learned with others? How much can you endure in the simple grind of life, of choosing to show up every day, not knowing, or even being unsure if that break will come, but trusting the fundamentals?

We often grow bored with the basics. We attempt, consciously or unconsciously, to make things more difficult, more complex with our fancy algorithms and stat sheets, thinking adulthood must somehow exclude grace and simplicity, that it can't be that easy.

Oh, but it can be.

Throughout my travels around the globe, first as a professional basketball player and now as an inspirational speaker, I have found the simple things are the most magical. Using the same skilled analytical eyes I applied toward the game of basketball, I now focus on the game of life.

How can I rebound? How can I help others rebound?

In returning to the basics and fundamentals and reframing them, I found the Seven Principles of Perseverance—the heart of this book.

In retrospect, because of these seven principles, I have won more times than I have lost, both on the basketball court and in life. In reevaluating so many old perceptions around words like *accountability* and *integrity*, I also found myself reexamining and redefining what it means to win, which led to understanding what it truly means to be an Alpha male in the twenty-first century.

So many men suffer in silent misery—like I did for so long—as the shifts in our world clash with our expectations of winning. Wasn't that what the American Dream was all about? Winning? But those days are gone.

I wrote this book for those men and for my son so they can know that while it is extremely painful, unsettling, and even lonely at times, the journey of authentic transformation into a New Alpha male offers more peace and clarity than any NBA contract.

1

WHAT IS A
NEW ALPHA MALE?

WE OFTEN DESCRIBE PEOPLE, especially men who dominate in sports, business, or any relationship, as "alpha." By our culture's standard, it could be argued there is nobody more alpha than a professional athlete. What more than sporting events brings all the other "alphas" in their fields—CEOs, musicians, actors, politicians, and social media celebrities—together in the same arena? Alpha culture idolizes the athlete—most people wish they too could hear people cheer their name as they compete and improvise for all the world to see.

The greatest athletes are not always the strongest, fastest, or the most talented: They are the ones who are the quickest to adapt to sudden changes in the game. Did the opposing team come out with a series of plays the scouting reports failed to predict? Did the opposing coach add an interesting wrinkle during a time-out? Did the refs change the way they were calling the game at halftime, or are they blatantly working against you? Most humans would cry foul, but the true Alpha adapts. He finds a way, even when the rules of the game shift.

Modern men are being asked to adapt to our changing world, yet many are fighting against it, still wanting to play by the old rules like "Be a tough guy" or "Man up" or "Bros before hoes." Nature offers no pity to those who cannot adapt—only extinction. It is not the strongest, fastest, or smartest who survive, but those who are most willing to rebound and evolve, on the basketball court and in life. And that is the New Alpha.

An Alpha is a winner. But what is winning?

REDEFINING WINNING

It is time to redefine "winning."

Most of us were conditioned to believe winning meant accruing trophies—championship rings, nuclear missiles, figures in our bank account, houses, cars, or wives. Winning meant people patting us on the back, telling us how awesome we were because we had the most, which made us the best. Winning was an external reward. It was superficial. It was fleeting.

In other words, winning was a chocolate Easter bunny: it looks so good, but crack it open, and it's hollow—it's *never* enough. We're hungry and unfulfilled, which leads us to overcompensate, posing as tough guys as we greedily scramble for the next prize because, on some level, we believe we live in a world of scarcity.

How does the New Alpha win? *Really* win?

By going against the grain. By doing things no one else is willing to do—things that cannot be measured on stat sheets. (Remember those bank shots?) By adapting. By doing something as crazy sounding as walking the path of the heart.

While "path of the heart" might sound a little too sappy and sweet, or even like a Hallmark special, it is anything but. The true path of the heart is gritty. It is being bold and willing to feel *all* that life throws at you and face everything with no distractions or avoidance mechanisms like stories, cultural clichés, or addictions, while remaining gentle, sometimes passive, and, most importantly, vulnerable. It's not an easy path.

As a boy in an ultrapatriarchal polygamist commune, I was taught that vulnerability meant weakness. Weakness meant danger because someone could take advantage of me. It meant women would feel I could not protect or provide for them. According to the skewed perspective of my upbringing, a real man, a manly man, could keep several women happy, not just one, while providing for and protecting them and all their many children. *Macho.*

Polygamy was said to be God's law, and only the most alpha men could fulfill it. We were taught we had to be tough guys to be loved, to rise above the crowd. Hard guys with puffed chests and brass belt buckles who were ready to die for our beliefs, ready for the government to swoop in at any moment and help us fulfill our self-fulfilling prophecies of martyrdom.

Polygamy or not, most men have been raised with a similar narrative—being vulnerable means someone manlier will triumph and you will be abandoned, isolated from the pack.

Through my old lens, foggy with patriarchy, if I wanted a woman to love me, I had to be that kind of alpha, a tough guy. If I wanted God to be proud of me, I had to be a winner. And so, at least by the standards my culture dictated, I became one: a gladiator.

Granted, I didn't slay the souls of the damned in a coliseum, wielding a sword while wearing a loin cloth. I did, however, run around half naked in shorts and a tank top, with a basketball in my hand in arenas all over the world. It was my job to defeat the man opposite me, to psychologically castrate him and possibly cause him to lose his job, thus taking away his alpha status. I wanted to destroy him not only physically and mentally but spiritually. I gave the crowds what they wanted—I decapitated souls as a proxy of rage. If I didn't, my opponents would.

I gave the crowds all that my body could give, entertaining them while hoping they would love and validate me, praying they would never forget me. Funny thing, though: most people didn't care about my feelings. There was no time for that—I was a gladiator. All they wanted to know was how I was going to amuse them or at least distract them from their own problems while I was sweating, bleeding, or worse.

If they didn't love me? I made sure they hated me so I could feed off their animosity. If they hated me enough, they would never forget me. Mission accomplished.

Yet, the "me" they loved or hated was whoever they projected me to be in any given arena on any given night. Sometimes I was a gladiator wearing the mask of a hero, and other nights, the villain. Believing the mask would earn me acceptance, happiness, and love, I wore it well. So well, in fact, I forgot who I truly was. Living in locker rooms for twenty years, all I knew was I was a male, a manly man—with a bleeding, broken heart, denying and obscuring parts of my essential self behind the facade of masculinity.

As I rose in the ranks of basketball, life continued to break me down. Time and again, I lost everything I had worked so hard to achieve, leaving me with nothing but my meretricious mask and a pattern of loss. I fought and I resisted, until every way I measured my material masculine worth was taken away. Ten years after my professional basketball career began, everything I had chased, all those trophies, external validations, and even my marriage, was gone. Even then, I fought tooth and nail to hold on to my masculinity—all I knew was to be a gladiator. It was my default. But when you are an aspiring motivational speaker staring at $27 in your bank account as a single father, living in a basement apartment as the living incarnation of Chris Farley's *Saturday Night Live* skit "Van Down by the River," you run out of denial tactics.

Maybe this gladiator myth wasn't as epic as I thought?

I had one option left: surrender. It was my only option, as I no longer liked who I saw reflected in all the tarnished trophies I'd accumulated.

With my only play left, I surrendered my dreams and stories and experienced true vulnerability. I learned that becoming humble wasn't shameful, but rather a bridge to knowing my own worth, the essence of Lance beneath the mask. I was winning at last.

Yes, I was a gladiator once—I was paid to destroy souls, and I did it well, but lost everything along the way. Now I am paid to help heal souls, and as a result, I heal my own.

COMMIT

Before an athlete can step into the arena, before we can strive to be Alpha, we must first make a commitment to ourselves, and then our coach (mentor or employer), teammates (coworkers or friends), and our family.

It's a commitment that becomes the default way of being, especially when doubt has you benched or defeated.

Here is *my* commitment to this work and to you: *I will create a safe space for men to go within and do the work of reframing assumptions we operate under as absolute truths, especially winning. I choose to be a bridge to enter a mind-set of spiritual development and genuine self-help.*

The work of spirituality and self-development is misguidedly believed to be solely a feminine domain. It is not. It demands bravery and a willingness to transcend our assumptions, our stories, our upbringing, even our cultural conditioning. To recognize and define our feelings; to find our self-worth from within, not through trophies, applause, or external rewards; and to speak our authentic truths. It is a domain that demands integration of our dark and light selves, our masculine and feminine.

When we do this, when we walk the path of the heart, we'll come to see that long-standing overriding masculine logic has run its course. There is power in acknowledging and unifying our masculine/feminine, dark/light energies that are within each of us. With this:

» A transmutation occurs when we empower ourselves with the accountability of choice.
» A steadiness develops when we move about the world with integrity.
» Prejudice dissolves and is replaced by healthy boundaries and ethical standards when we face the world with compassion.

As we take this journey to becoming New Alpha males together, I will show you:

» The necessity of discomfort, detours, and broken dreams in your path of life.
» The grace that is found when you accept and surrender to forces beyond your physical and logical control.
» The true freedom that is discovered when you transform into a leader of your own life.
» The clarity and gratitude that is received when you are brave enough to forgive.

And finally, that winning is *intimacy*.

Not the Hollywood version of intimacy but a true intimacy, which is self-intimacy.

Self-intimacy is where I found my worth by rewiring the thought patterns I'd inherited that said intimacy was a destination high, a reward for a role well played, a mythical soul mate to read my mind so I wouldn't have to be vulnerable and communicate. With self-intimacy comes consistency of character, resilience, and endurance in the face of external pressures asking you to compromise yourself.

Before we go further, read this aloud:

I commit to walk a new path of authentic Alpha vulnerability, no matter how scary, uncomfortable, or unsettling it might be.

Write those twenty-one words down and sign your name below them. Seriously, sign it. The tough guy act doesn't fly here. It is easy to puff your chest with bravado, to roll your eyes, or to dismiss something as beneath you. Anyone can do that. But is it brave? No.

Let's drop the pretenses. This is not a time for machismo. This is a safe space without judgment or shame.

HARD TO GUARD

I was selected as a captain for most of the basketball teams I played on due to my ability to read body language, no matter the country or culture. I always watched and studied people. As I developed and expanded my game, I not only adopted tactics from what my peers did but would observe and ask, "What *aren't* they doing?"

If everyone is trying to dunk and block shots, this creates a concentration of teammates vying for the same playing time, the same role, the same space on the court. Rather than trying to compete and be one of many, I sought out other ways to play, to fill in spots where I could score readily, where people weren't used to guarding. I learned to outrun everyone for easy layups, unlike most centers who were used to brute force matches of post-ups and drop steps near the basket, where you jockey for angle and position like sumo wrestlers.

I also set screens to get my teammates open and then popped into the open pockets near the three-point line where I could shoot my bank shots. Setting a screen for someone else, attempting to get them open, got me more open. If you aren't picking up on the metaphor, I will spell it out for you: when you attempt to help and serve others, you will help yourself, possibly even more than those you are serving.

Furthermore, as a right-handed player, I learned to score more with my left hand than my right. The universe doesn't suffer one-dimensional folks well because life is anything but one-dimensional. To extend my career, I focused on becoming ambidextrous and cerebral, and because opposing players had little experience guarding that, I became hard to guard, and therefore, valuable.

Not only did I observe one-dimensional patterns in opposing players, but I began to observe a deeper pattern in opposing coaches, and even some of my own coaches. The pattern was fear. Fear rooted in a belief that control, or the *illusion* of control, would keep them from losing. This is where most teams fall apart, usually at the hands of insecure executives who never played basketball but think their MBA and advanced algorithms can measure heart.

Do you know what is truly weak? The inability to adapt.

So many researchers and self-help authors are trying to quantify the human heart with logic and statistics, all of which feed into the corporate mentality of CEOs and front-office sports executives who think they can measure chemistry, intuition, experience, and passion through stat sheets. This is the brain thinking it is superior to the heart. The brain is logic, and the heart is intuition. We cannot quantify heart. It defies logic. It is eternal.

All the great athletes who ascended to their summits of glory did so not because of their logical minds or a gift for crunching the numbers, but because of their presence and trust in their bodies, the flowing from their heart of pure intuition, instinct, and presence in the moment. The greats became the greats—in the arena, the boardroom, the concert hall, the lecture hall, or the ER—by walking the path of the heart, not by head alone.

While the world cheers the exalted athlete, it often fails to see the lesson said athlete is teaching in the moment, which is the importance and application of instinct and intuition, of heart. Ironically, the CEOs will cheer the athlete from their front-row seats for making a great instinctive play yet go to the office the next day and hamstring their employees with spreadsheets, trying to win the game through logic and research data, by playing not to lose.

The greats play to win.

Athletes sense vulnerability and lick their chops when they see an opponent is clearly no longer in their bodies but are lost in their heads. You can see it when basketball players step to the free-throw line to shoot—are they in their head? If so, they will likely miss the shot, like I nearly did when I accidentally banked in my free throw in Cleveland. When I tried to play basketball from my head, from logic, I was at my weakest. When I played from my heart, not my head, and instead trusted my intuition, is when I was strongest—hard to guard.

This applies to life. When your default is to always rely on the mind first to process information before allowing yourself to make a move, you will become predictable and possibly one step behind; instinct is quicker. Walking the path of the heart is being in your body, feeling and trusting all of what your intuition is telling you, while still allowing the logic of memory and experience to have a proper place but not drive the machine. When we walk the path of the heart, we see the opportunity to be more at peace and present in our bodies as we maneuver through life. We have the opportunity to be a different kind of leader who leads in humility and empowered action, not reaction—a new kind of Alpha male who leads through compassion, not intimidation.

"But Lance," I hear you say, "The old model of leadership works!"

That old leadership model of authoritarianism worked when there was no mandate or social media to enforce transparency and there were more employees than jobs, but recent surveys by the US Bureau of Labor Statistics show we live in a world where there are more jobs than employees, especially in the technology sector. This has shifted the power dynamic to the employees, yet so many bosses refuse to accept this because they want to retain absolute power, which they were taught to strive for, which promised them alpha status.

"It's my turn now!" they say with anger, shaming the younger generations as weak because coaches and bosses can't verbally abuse them anymore.

Do you know what is truly weak? The inability to adapt.

By watching so many coaches and people in leadership fail to lead with humility and take responsibility, I saw stubbornness, insecurity, pride, and fear as the ingredients of their undoing. While many of my coaches were stubborn, few of them were perseverant.

Stubbornness is the inability to adapt; perseverance is the ability to adapt.

The Seven Principles of Perseverance I share in this book—Accountability, Integrity, Compassion, Discomfort, Acceptance, Transformation, and Forgiveness and Gratitude—are not the result of a fancy statistical algorithm or magic spell.

"But, Lance, I already know those things, you aren't teaching me anything new."

Remember, integrity was one of Enron's corporate values. People love paying lip service to these fundamentals, but do they take the time to clarify what they mean and, furthermore, accomplish them? The Seven Principles of Perseverance are simple-yet-difficult daily choices that force us out of our comfort zones toward unity with our authentic self, where peace and clarity hold more value than money or fleeting praise. In that space of clarity, true leadership on your own terms is established.

This is Alpha.

. . .

Before we can delve into the Seven Principles of Perseverance and start the game, we have to warm up. We have to break down the bad habits and rewire our brains to change how we process information. We have to undo stale thought patterns that no longer serve us. We have to shine a light on our blind spots, especially the things we've assumed are absolute truths, which, well, *aren't*, particularly when it comes to the lessons and lies of our culture, our personal fears, the stories we tell ourselves, the addictions that keep us stuck, and our unrealistic projections.

We have to revisit our foundation and possibly rebuild it, ripping out the bad habits that no longer serve us. All basketball players develop bad habits, but the best ones are able to break them down to their basics and then reconstruct them on a new foundation as they adapt in this game of life.

Let's warm up.

2

WARM-UP AND (UN)TRAINING

AT THE AGE OF FIVE, in the polygamous commune where I grew up, I had a Sunday school teacher impress upon me that God had made me deaf as a form of punishment. I never asked my parents if this explanation was true, because I feared they might say yes. I kept the story hidden so deeply it embedded into my subconscious and became a major operating glitch within the faulty mechanism that is my brain. Consequently, I had a warped perception of God and my self-worth as a boy, driven by the belief I had to atone for a past sin I could not recollect. And so whatever ill treatment came my way, I rationalized that I deserved it.

Oh, the stories we tell about ourselves and others, to ourselves and others! Stories we believe are truth. And we hold onto stories no matter how badly the hot coal burns, because we believe they are our identity. Our merit badges. Stories hurt worse than physical pain, or at least my stories did and still do on days when I choose to hold onto them.

I inherited the martyrdom archetype, or persona, from my cultural upbringing—my grandfather was imprisoned by the US government for practicing polygamy, only to be assassinated later at the order of the head of a rival sect. This not only shaped my community and family stories of martyrdom but helped shape and solidify my own early personal stories, framed in the same fear that God had made me deaf as punishment.

We tell ourselves and each other stories to perpetuate and reaffirm other stories. The brain is a magnet for them, creating what we individually call our reality or our paradigm. For most of us, that paradigm operates on a foundation of fear that we will be abandoned by our loved ones. We fear we will be rejected by our community or our culture, and for most children and adults, there are few things more frightening than not belonging.

When it came to making it into the NBA, I had many reasons and inspirations: love of the game, financial security, praise, accomplishment, spite (I love proving people wrong), the hope to inspire others with disabilities, and last but not least, fear. Fear that I would never be good enough. Fear that a woman would never want me. Fear that God would reject me. Fear that I would be abandoned and tortured in Hell. As I grew older and went to college and began to travel the world, my fear of an actual Hell began to diminish, but the other fears remained, further solidifying the paradigm that was so deeply embedded in the processing core of my brain, which said I had to earn love. This story of fear also triggered an addiction within me—addiction to approval and validation as I projected fear onto the world in codependent "nice guy" behavior. Funny thing, though: it wasn't until I was about thirty when I finally asked myself, "Lance, do you know this story of God punishing you to be true?"

My job as an adult was to question and, furthermore, challenge this foundation of reality from which I had been operating my entire life.

That is your job as well. The details of our stories may not be the same, but we all share patterns of culture, fear, addiction, and projection.

WARM-UP 1: CULTURE

While playing basketball on every continent on the globe, I observed a prevalent flaw through every culture: self-lionization.

"Our country is the best."

"Our community's values are the best values."

"Our basketball league is the toughest league in the world."

During my travels, culture has always fascinated me. I smile when people label other groups as "cults" yet are unwilling to look at their own similarities and parallels. Based on my experience of living in one, I'd define a cult or cult mentality as: *Seeing and hearing only the things you want or have been conditioned to see and hear.*

By my definition, we can look at not only extreme religious sects but major religions as well, along with team sports, political parties, corporations, nationalism, and prejudices. Seeing and hearing only the things you want to see and hear, or cult mentality, is a global phenomenon we inoculate from scrutiny, even self-scrutiny, by labeling it as belief.

For many of us, beliefs are nothing more than comfort zones, as we are afraid of the unknown. Self-aggrandizement is how we rationalize our comfort zones (disguised as beliefs) when we are too afraid to step beyond them. We want to feel safe and so willingly put ourselves in constricting boxes that are our beliefs. We take this ever further, making the self-imposed restriction of our beliefs and stories worthwhile by saying they make us special. For example, "I live in the greatest country in the world; I don't need to travel abroad" is a mind-set that prevents so much life experience in seeing what the world has to offer.

My job as an adult was to question and, furthermore, challenge this foundation of reality from which I had been operating my entire life.

"We are the *true* church."

"Americans are all fat, entitled, spoiled brats."

The great humor of it is, if everyone's values and beliefs are the best, then they negate each other.

One day while sitting in an airplane, looking down at the earth below, it occurred to me that the human brain is like an empty hard drive—the ones you see in the stores when you are building your own computer from scratch. When we are born, we are a clean hard drive, an empty slate, each being slightly different due to nature. And the culture we are born into is the software operating system, like Microsoft, Linux, or Mac, which processes our values, prejudices, stories, and biases, and is installed on that hard drive. This algorithm is then nurtured within us as "truth."

Microsoft does not compute with the same values and algorithms as Linux or Mac, yet we impose our values and viruses on others, wondering, "Why isn't their Microsoft brain computing and registering my Macintosh values equally and in the same way? Obviously, they must be an inferior operating system, because my system is the best!"

Our values may be logic based, yet so much of our logic stems from our culture and family, which allows many of us to believe our own individual values are superior and, furthermore, that our logic is sound. In fact, logic is probably the greatest blind spot we have because we live in a time when logic and reason are no longer synonymous. Anyone can "logic" themselves into believing they are right and they know the truth. The human brain is capable of all sorts of mental gymnastics and cognitive dissonance to stay secure within its paradigm of familiarity and importance, like blaming immigrants for taking our jobs, then turning around and shopping at big-box stores selling imported goods that are the consequence of exported jobs. Logic is simply what all brains do to make themselves believe they are in control.

Reason is different.

Reason is understanding that everyone has their own logic. It is understanding that truth is in the space between everyone's logic, in the shades of gray between the polarizing extremes of conservative and liberal or patriarchy versus feminism. Believing we have absolute truth is not reasonable. Saying "I can't do that because it is against my religion" is reasonable toward the logic of others. Whereas "You can't do that because it is against my religion" is unreasonable toward the logic of others. When logic is no longer reasonable to the logic of others, it is not only unreasonable—it is irrational.

If there were a one-size-fits-all system of values, humankind would have found it by now. Yet we make the erroneous assumption that every other brain/operating system automatically has identical wiring and operates as such. This explains our shock and horror when someone inadvertently insults our values, and further enrages us when they show no remorse or even awareness they did it.

Dissecting our culture can be unsettling but necessary as we undo the bad habits of assumed beliefs that may have served us but are now keeping us in a feedback loop of increasing stagnation. As you will see, our inherited culture can be one of the easiest and most essential "motherboards" to rewire, for once we begin to do it, it will broaden our reality exponentially, so much so that we begin to see the world differently. And from that new perspective, while uncomfortable at first, we will begin to find growth and new experiences that provide more information about who we truly are underneath the old cultural mask we wore to belong.

Do the Work

Your first warm-up before game time is to understand your cultural programming, from the micro expanding into the macro. Start by objectively listing the logic-based values and biases of the immediate culture in which you were nurtured—your family, religion, or community. Once you have that, compute the values of the geographic region you're from. Finally, examine the values of your country.

Here are some of my responses:

Immediate Culture: *Mormon Fundamentalism*
1. We are God's chosen people.
2. Ours is the only path to salvation.
3. We are elite, over all the nonbelievers and even other Christians.
4. Be vigilant, because you never know how the Devil may tempt you.
5. I may have to die for my beliefs.
6. I am a victim—the world is against me and my community.
7. I am flawed and sinful.
8. Love must be earned.
9. Follow the rules; don't ask questions.
10. Only men may speak to and for God in our patriarchal culture.
11. Success is marked by having many wives, and the more I have, the more spiritual I am.

Regional Values: *Montana*

1. Pull yourself up by the bootstraps.
2. No handouts; earn your way.
3. No whining or complaining.
4. Help others who are stranded at the side of the road.
5. Wave to other drivers.
6. The government can't be trusted . . .
7. . . . but, we're still the greatest country in the world.
8. 'Merica . . .
9. Be polite and friendly at all times . . . until someone tries to take your guns away.
10. Success is a huge log-cabin home, with a bunch of horses and a massive pickup truck, an ATV, snowmobile, and a white buffalo head mounted over the fireplace.

National Values: *United States*

1. America is the greatest power in the world.
2. We are the beacon of democracy.
3. God bless America!
4. We believe in liberty, but . . .
5. . . . freedom isn't free.
6. When all else fails, litigate.
7. Happy Hollywood endings are to be expected because . . .
8. . . . the American Dream is real!
9. I am entitled to said American Dream.
10. Success or winning can be measured by wealth, influence, and a beautiful woman on my arm.

These values are the bells and whistles on your fancy computer.

When you do this warm-up, you might find yourself asking "How many of these values are mine?" Did you consciously choose them, or did you assume they were truth and allow them to set in your subconscious from which you processed the world based on your various experiences?

We think these values are our identity, but I promise you, they are not. At least not our *soul* identity, by which I mean who we truly are in the eternal spheres beyond this matrix board that is our Earth dimension and the avatars we are playing in it.

As we begin to break down the framework of logic we both built and inherited from our culture, from the micro (immediate) to the macro (national) it will be uncomfortable, and if you feel that, you are on the right path and are doing "the work." Simply put, you know you are doing the work if you are uncomfortable, as that is where growth is, and in the discomfort of the new and unfamiliar space, your true identity—your soul identity—will emerge.

That's when the true work can commence. Remember, this is a warm-up. Grab some paper or a notebook and see for yourself.

Immediate Culture:
    1.
    2.
    3.
    4.
    5.

Regional Values:
    1.
    2.
    3.
    4.
    5.

National Values:
    1.
    2.
    3.
    4.
    5.

Now, fill out your list again, but this time do your best to put yourself in the other gender's shoes. Be sure to list the definition of success and winning in each subset of culture.

Did you ever consciously choose these values? Do you now?

As you begin to dissect your culture, you will be surprised at how much tribal mentality exists around you, on the news, on social media, at work, among people feeling their need to be on the "right" side and play a role to fit in on that team. It's likely you will find a strange calm come over you when you realize you don't have to play that game anymore.

In our attachment to our culture, we become inured to our roles and our familiarity in those roles. Our culture drives so much of our fear: fear of other cultures impinging on our beliefs, land, resources, and bank accounts; fear of being kicked out of our culture and community or ostracized. Simply being aware of the blind spots within your culture will give you a massive advantage in the game of life, as you will be playing self-aware while most others are playing self-absorbed. (More about this later.)

WARM-UP 2: FEAR

A recurring theme that transcends all cultures I've witnessed in my travels is that humans operate in two modes: trust/love or fear. Most of us operate in fear—fear that we will not be good enough, that we will fail, that love will be withheld, that we will be abandoned, which is most often the underlying fear in everyone's behavior.

Fear is the opposite of trust/love and creates uncertainties, insecurities, and trust issues, which are the ingredients of self-fulfilling prophecies. An example of a self-fulfilling prophecy I experienced firsthand is the belief that my grandfather was killed because this world isn't a safe place. Even the government can't be trusted; thus, we should continue to live on the outskirts of society as outlaws. Once we break enough rules, the government will come and arrest us, thereby confirming that the government is against us.

My logic was fear based. Rather than choosing an alternative scenario that maybe my grandfather *wasn't* a prophet, which would initiate a whole new fear that suggested I wasn't special (as I faced later in life), as a child I chose to fit into the community and believe that my grandfather was a literal martyr. That came at the cost of believing this world was not a safe place. We all put ourselves in this kind of ridiculous predicament through our stories.

A common example of a self-fulfilling prophecy might be "My parents abandoned me; people always leave," and so I will attract partners who I will continually engage in "hot and cold" behavior with. I even assign them traits they don't really have, confusing and frustrating them to the point that they will leave, confirming my belief that people always leave.

Most people, especially when they are behaving badly, are coming from a place of fear. Even if they are acting grandiose and superior to others, this behavior can be rooted in a fear that they are not important, and so need people to see them as important; otherwise they will be abandoned. Ironically, this creates the self-fulfilling prophecy of abandonment, because eventually everyone gets tired of a diva, and they leave.

I operated from fear most of my life, and I still do some days when I'm on autopilot. My biggest fear is abandonment. Where I grew up, the threat of hell felt very real, where I would be abandoned by God and my loved ones, entrapped forever in a dark place where I would be humiliated and tormented by Satan and his minions for all eternity. Laugh all you want at the silliness of the notion, but that was a real fear for me as a boy.

No matter how it manifests, most of us operate from fear.

Do the Work

Your work here is to list your fears and a coping mechanism. Beyond abandonment, some other common fears are powerlessness and humiliation. Humiliation is actually a second-tier fear, as it leads to either abandonment or powerlessness. But we will work with these three:

1. Abandonment
2. Powerlessness
3. Humiliation

I'll start: I fear *failure* because it will lead to *abandonment*, and I cope with it *by working way too much and not enjoying life*.

Your turn.

I fear:

_____ because it will lead to _____ and I cope with it by _____.

_____ because it will lead to _____ and I cope with it by _____.

_____ because it will lead to _____ and I cope with it by _____.

Assess your answers. Which childhood fears still drive you as an adult? Do these old operating patterns still serve you?

Be real with yourself. Honestly evaluating your fears is a wonderful way to create intimacy with yourself. When you feel anxiety come up, it's an indicator that fear is triggering it, so allow yourself the space to pause and create a place of ease for yourself, asking "What fear is this anxiety coming from? Abandonment? Powerlessness?"

Once you can do this with yourself, it is easier to share it with your significant others, helping them understand the real you behind the mask. This leads to true intimacy. And in true intimacy, we are not afraid of others leaving us if they don't like all the fears and stories we are working through, because we now have intimacy with ourselves, and that is more fulfilling than any outside relationship.

You no longer need other people to heal your stories. That's your job.

WARM-UP 3: STORIES

A story is a perspective, a way we choose to narrate a fear, event, memory, or hope. While a perspective might provide a relative truth, it is not an absolute truth.

Remember how I believed the story of God punishing me by making me deaf? That's one example of a relative truth that I believed to be an absolute truth.

Another is a story that plagued me for years—that men in power in our polygamist sect had more wives because they were better men and that was how God validated them. A woman was the measurement of a man, so more wives = more blessings = more power = more wives = more blessings, and so on. No one ever said this outright, but as a boy raised in a linear-thinking, cause-and-effect world and doing my best to make sense of it, this narration made things quite simple and logical.

Even after I left the sect, the story that the best ("alpha") man always got the best girl as a sign of God's validation continued in my subconscious well into my thirties. Consequently, I found many women to date who allowed me to sustain and confirm my imagined stories and deepest fears that I was not man enough and did not deserve love. The human brain is a fascinating machine—we find people to fit our perspectives, people who will play the roles we need them to play to allow us to remain in our stories and paradigms.

Can you imagine how much baggage this old story of my worth as a man being attached to a woman's love emerged in my marriage? How it was amplified when I was going through our divorce and when the mother of my son was now with another man? It was the most painful experience of my life. It was more painful than the loss of my NBA dream and all the stories attached to my basketball career. It struck the deepest fear from my childhood and story that said I would be abandoned, that I was not man enough for God or a woman.

It took everything I had—all the emotional and psychological coping skills I acquired from my experiences—to grieve and work through that old story, the loss of our marriage, and how I was responsible on my end for the self-fulfilling prophecy I was now living in.

When I was coming through the wreckage of my divorce, my default victim/martyr mode tried to protect me. The martyr story is an old coping mechanism from childhood that allowed me to process why bad things happen: God is punishing/testing me. As a child it served a purpose—it helped me make sense of a crazy world—but those stories and default operating modes no longer empowered me. They had become patterns of loss and provided neither relief nor reward. That's when I realized I had only one option: to peel away all the roles I had been conditioned to play by my family, community, and culture and create a new operating protocol for my brain.

It was my job as an adult and a disciplined athlete to use the skills my mentors and coaches taught me on the physical plane and apply them to the psychological and spiritual dimension. Once I began to attempt to let go of the stories, my ego fought back and made my life even more miserable, as if the universe was asking me to "prove" I wanted to let them go. I had to make a choice: go back to my default, safety mode—my martyrdom reality—or continue to brave serious discomfort into a realm where there are no old stories to help me process the world. I made my choice. I would begin to see the world in a new way, as an empowered and accountable adult.

We will begin by assessing the stories we most commonly tell others—those are the easy ones to spot and work with. Then we'll start to question the lens of how you are telling those stories. Are you telling the story through the narrative of a child? Of a victim? Or are you choosing to tell the story from the lens of an empowered teacher? That is your choice. Every time.

Do the Work

Organize your "library" of stories and consider which ones are still serving you and which should be untold.

» Which stories were coping mechanisms in your youth that helped process negative experiences? Are they still serving that function?

» Recall the most important story—it could be traumatic or mundane—that laid a subconscious foundation of "truth" that still trips you up. Perhaps it is a truth your family or culture imparted on you that no longer serves you.

» What basic fear is triggering this story? Abandonment? Powerlessness? Humiliation? Maybe even pain?

» Ask yourself: "Do I know this story to be true?" What is your answer?

» Which narrative persona—the victim or teacher—is telling the story?

» Do this with five or more familiar stories (not the funny ones) you like to share with the world to allow them to get to know you. How many of them are empowered? How many are victimizing?

A quick action would be to list on a whiteboard or a piece of paper all the stories that you have told yourself and others. By learning to be aware of your stories, you become self-aware of every time you want to tell them, and you ask yourself in that awareness, what am I hoping to gain from the telling of the story?

WARM-UP 4: ADDICTION

Often, to release the pressure on our psyches from the stories we haven't or can't let go of, we create coping mechanisms—rituals or habits that manage stress, discomfort, or other manifestations of fear. Most often, addiction is the coping mechanism within us that overpowers all the others. It becomes the symptom of our underlying stories and fears. We all suffer from addiction, it's just that some addictions are more culturally acceptable.

I am a recovering addict—seeking approval and validation is my drug.

Unable to play basketball with my hearing aids in, I couldn't always hear what praises or obscenities the crowds called my way. However, I could read their lips, and more importantly, I could read what their body language was telling me. My hearing loss makes me more empathic, as my sense of feel is sharpened, yet I was a closet empath. People couldn't know I had feelings—who had time for that? Remember, I was a gladiator.

As a closet empath, standing in the middle of arenas, I could always feel the rage along with the hopes and dreams of the crowd, and I often got lost, not in the noise, but in the energy and cascade of emotions with their accompanying stories and fears.

Not only was I a closet empath, I was a codependent empath, and I fed off their emotions. Especially their praise. I needed it. Really needed it. Their adoration was my addiction.

I believed if I could do enough, the fans would love me. I could make them see I was a good person, that I had value. I craved their validation. And through that need, that addiction, that fear, I destroyed, decapitated, my soul. I was more vicious toward myself than toward any of my opponents.

This addiction ruined my happiness, yet I could not get enough of it. I hated needing and wanting people to validate me, but it felt so good when I got it—my fix.

I loathed that people thought they could judge my value by looking at my stat sheet if I had a bad night on the basketball court, yet I loved it when people looked at my stat sheet on a good night and patted me on the back and told me "Good job!" This triggered a release of dopamine—the hormone in our brains that rewards us with feelings of pleasure and satisfaction yet is also the hormone of addiction.

What happened when I didn't get praise after a bad game, if I was unable to get the dopamine release? Mr. Hyde came out, and I would brood through the night.

My addiction began as a coping skill to cover my fear of abandonment, and it ended up failing me, sabotaging both personal and professional relationships in my adult life. The need for praise was a superficial pacifier that told me I was a good person and I wouldn't be abandoned. It soon grew into an addiction, a coping tool that turned cancerous yet was only a symptom, or a mask hiding a greater fear: that I would be abandoned, powerless, or humiliated.

I also had an addiction to prayer, which I now know to be a classified illness called scrupulosity. I would sneak out of class and pray several times a day, asking God to not be angry with me. I kept this secret for years until I finally went on medication when I was twenty-one. The medication kept the anxiety at bay, but the fear was still there, lurking beneath the surface. When I learned to combat my story, asking if it was true, my addiction to prayer, like my need for approval, faded.

Where many rehab efforts fall short is in their overzealous attack of the symptom, the addictive behavior, rather than the story and fear triggering the addiction. We can't heal the wounded heart through the mind. The mind and mental medication can help us cope with the wounding of the heart, but we must heal the heart with the heart by being brave enough to open our hearts back up.

Heal your stories with heart, and you will alleviate the pressure and need for the addiction.

What is your addiction? While it is easy to shame the use of drugs, alcohol, and pornography for the visible compulsions they are, there are countless other forms, such as:

» Approval—*How many likes and followers do I have? How much applause did I get?*

» Codependency—*Seeking approval through fixing other people's problems as a way to avoid your own.*
» Food—*Eating to distract yourself from other stories and fears.*
» Devices like phones or computers—*Addiction allows us to avoid engaging with other people.*
» Religion/Piety/Self-Righteousness—*Trusting that your God is the best god and will take care of everything, so you don't have to do any work or introspection or accountability for your part in relationships and experiences.*
» Control—*Needing to control other people or the world around you because you don't want them to see that you're not perfect.*
» Perfection—*Needing your life to look or be perfect because you can't imagine yourself having any worth if that's not the case.*
» Competition—*A strain of perfectionism and approval. Always having to "win."*
» Compulsive Shopping, Hoarding, Consumerism—*Another form of control fostering the illusion that if we have enough, we will be enough.*
» Socializing—*Seeking out human company and avoiding solitude because we can't stand to be alone with our thoughts of low self-esteem.*
» Information—*Always having to be the one who knows, the smartest person in the room, which is a strain of both approval and control addictions.*
» Gossip—*By diminishing others we believe we are elevating ourselves.*

I could go on, but the point is we all have coping mechanisms, and the ones that serve us without harming others are useful, but when we rely on any of them to the detriment of our well-being or the well-being of those around us, it becomes an addiction.

Do the Work

It's time to get brutally honest with yourself. Let go of blaming anyone for why you have chosen to do the things you have done in your life, let go of judgment, and identify which addictions have driven your operating system. You may have only one or two, or you may have several.

1. List your addictions and coping mechanisms.
2. Label them with the fears you are protecting yourself from via your addictions.
3. Add the stories that arise from those fears that trigger your addictions.
4. Finally, what is the reward the addiction is giving you? The addiction is giving something, most likely distraction, an escape from a story; otherwise, you wouldn't have an addiction as there would be no payoff.

Addiction	Fear	Story	Reward
_____	_____	_____	_____
_____	_____	_____	_____
_____	_____	_____	_____

As you list addictions, you will be able to consciously observe them. Owning them is a huge step, and if you want to stay in denial, this book isn't for you. As you own your addictions, when you feel the need to engage in the behavior, you can now ask yourself: What anxiety is being triggered that I am now in need of this distraction/addiction? Furthermore, what fear is triggering this anxiety?

A potential action might be to begin to welcome other coping mechanisms that you know have a fighting chance to compete with your main addiction/coping mechanism. Make a game plan on a piece of paper by writing down what your replacement coping mechanism will be whenever the urge to fall back into a place of addiction arises.

WARM-UP 5: PROJECTION

We loathe in others what we hate most and often deny about ourselves.

This is called projection.

Think about it—the insults people hurl at each other are often the labels they find most terrifying. This was clear to me during the year following my release from the NBA. I was playing in the NBA minor leagues and not in a good state of mind. I was depressed; I was angry; I felt worthless. I believed I had failed. I had no value to offer the world. My erroneous story attached my human worth to a material outcome.

In that minor-league locker room I had a teammate, a rookie, whose insecurity was so clear to me—and I hated it because it mirrored my insecurities and made me uncomfortable. Eventually, there was a blowup. I was feeling so worthless that I unleashed my fear on this teammate. Never before have I ever been so vocally venomous toward another human being. I was loud—yelling, screaming, and personal. I cut right to the bone, because I knew exactly what to say—the things that would have hurt me the most to hear. He was the mirror into which I reflected my own projections, but it wasn't about him. It was me, lashing at me, and I hated him for reflecting my insecurities.

In my rage, I couldn't see at the time that he was a mirror for my own self-loathing. I hated in him the same insecurities I hated in myself. It was only after I lashed out and had time to cool off that I began to break down and sob. I was able to apologize to him later, but so many hurtful things had been said, I wondered if I could ever take them back. I hope my teammate reads this book and will allow me to find him to have a good talk, expressing so much gratitude for the beautiful mirror he was. That is my true wish.

Nobody is exempt: we loathe in others what we hate most about ourselves.

Think of who triggers you. What about them irritates you? Maybe you have a relative who is a know-it-all and is condescending, and you can't stand being around them during family get-togethers? Is their "know-it-all-ness" a cover for their own insecurities? Although it may manifest in a different way, are you guilty of insecurity as well, which is why this makes you uncomfortable?

Again, when people judge and label you, they're using the same label they are terrified of being labeled.

"Oh, he's so soft—too sensitive." *I hope no one calls me soft! I don't want people to see I have vulnerability . . .*

"She's so dense!" *I hope no one finds out I don't understand what's being discussed . . .*

Think back on the gossip and judgment you have ever heard or engaged in. The people casting judgment would have been terrified to be labeled and judged for things they shamed another for doing. This is often manifested in the behavior of hypocrisy, when someone's fear of being caught for a social wrong is so great they project that shame onto another, hoping they are never shamed.

Taking this even further, if you have ever been physically, mentally, or sexually assaulted, you were prey for someone who felt they had no power. They had a fear they were powerless, and unless they dominated someone else, they felt they would be dominated. They attempted to dominate you so they could feel powerful instead of powerless.

This does not mean we condone or allow assault and abusive behavior to occur. Never. We must always force accountability, as that is one of the greatest acts of unconditional love when we provide a mirror for others to learn about themselves. And in that act, we are able to see our own reflections and the lessons they are helping us learn about ourselves as we ask, "How is this experience helping me for my highest good? Is it allowing the trauma of abuse to be channeled to hold even deeper compassion for others who have been abused?"

Doing the work is self-reflection and the accountability for all your thoughts and masks that you wear as well as the roles you play to belong. I have seen people who will go into the deepest, darkest jungles of the Amazon before they would dare to go into the deepest, darkest parts of their own selves, confirming that their fearless excursions in the physical world are nothing more than distraction—and possibly even addiction.

Do the Work

First: Think and write about a time when someone judged you. Was what they judged you for something they would have been terrified to be labeled as? Draw up the memory and recall it. Reframe it, realizing it was not about you but their own internal fears that they, too, might be humiliated, abandoned, or entrapped.

Second: Think and write about a time you judged, gossiped about, or shamed someone. While it may not be for the same action, was the underlying fear or cause of behavior something you were guilty of as well?

If you can, reach out to this person and write them an empowered letter of gratitude, thanking them for the opportunity they provided you to learn more about yourself. Hopefully, in your own human error, you provided them opportunity to learn about themselves as well.

CURRENT BOX SCORE

Place all your culture, fears, stories, addictions, and projections into their respective stat lines so they are exposed and hard to ignore, like a current box score. Don't judge or shame them. Store them in a place in your mind that is visible, but far enough away so that you can see them objectively whenever I reference these terms throughout the rest of the book. We'll be processing them as we continue on our journey to Alpha, applying them to the Seven Principles of Perseverance:

The Seven Principles of Perseverance

1. Accountability
2. Integrity
3. Compassion
4. Discomfort
5. Acceptance
6. Transformation
7. Forgiveness and Gratitude

GAME TIME

(3)

ACCOUNTABILITY

The First Principle of Perseverance

BEFORE THE GAME EVEN STARTS, I feel the earth quake as thousands of people stomp their feet in sync with a ritualistic chant. They've been doing so for hours. Even if I could hear the words they are screaming, I wouldn't be able to understand them, as I don't speak the language here in Turkey. I can practically smell the adrenaline and aggression, along with the bonfire in the middle of the crowd, but the strongest sensation is the pent-up rage of grudges that go back lifetimes.

Rage . . . so much rage.

Instead of attacking each other, the throng has proxies: the athletes on the basketball court who represent their culture, pride, values, losses, sorrows, and fears. Then, as the ref blows the whistle, someone with impeccable aim launches a double-A battery from the stands, and it clips the side of my head. I show no sign of irritation, because that would only entertain them.

As the ball is tipped, the chants never pause. The feet never stop stomping. The rage never ceases raging. Although I can't really hear, I feel everything, as my other senses are on hyperalert. I see every nuance of body movement as I stare in soft focus to observe my surroundings with expanded peripheral vision. I read my teammates' positions, which on days like this one are essential to figuring out what play I will run on offense because our coach is too paranoid to use hand signals for fear the other team will be able to interpret them. Although I could argue with the coach and tell him he is being ridiculous, the twenty-four-second shot clock only allows for so much brilliance, and the defense *always* has to give us something. I know the coach is too engulfed in fear to receive any feedback, so I have to read the teammates and adapt to the plays they are running.

Except this time, I get it wrong.

The ball whizzes past my head from a pass I am not prepared for and sails out of bounds. Turnover. The crowd erupts. The coach falls to the floor in an overly demonstrative plea for mercy to whatever gods may hear him, but that is, in reality, a deflection to absolve himself of accountability, letting the owners see it isn't his fault, but rather a player's fault. *My* fault.

The coach demands a timeout.

"Lance, that's not the play I called!" he screams. "Are you stupid?"

You have a choice in such moments, a choice you have been faced with many times before. You can either say, "Hey, yo, coach! You're being ridiculous by not using hand signals. No one can hear—not just me," or you can say, "You're right, coach. I screwed up the play."

I choose the latter, as I have time and again.

Why? Because when I was ejected from my first basketball game at the age of fourteen, the ref thought I was ignoring him when I couldn't hear him. That was when everyone began doubting if I could play basketball, so I made a choice: *I am never going to use my hearing as an excuse, because excuses would prove my doubters right.*

When you have had contracts overseas withdrawn after coaches and owners found out you had hearing loss, when you have had a lover leave you for someone wealthier, when you have had a mentor betray you, you can take the route of being a victim or you can empower yourself. I chose to never be anyone's target. I knew the world was never going to stop and start at my convenience or accommodate my hearing loss on the basketball court—that's entitlement and the antithesis of accountability. I knew if I wanted the world to adapt to me, I had to adapt to the world, owning my limitations along the way.

This ownership and adaptation is *accountability*.

DEFINING ACCOUNTABILITY

Accountability is the first and most crucial of the Seven Principles of Perseverance and the strongest characteristic of emotional wellness and health. Accountability, like the first quarter of a basketball game, establishes the environment and tempo for becoming a New Alpha. Without it, the subsequent principles are worthless.

We set the tone with accountability.

It is the source from which all the other principles grow. When I say accountability, I mean responsibility not only for actions but thoughts, reactions, projections, and emotions as well. Furthermore, accountability applies to the thought patterns and stories we tell ourselves.

The concepts of emotional intelligence, empathy, and emotional health are abstract notions. What are the criteria by which we measure them?

Simple: accountability.

Staying accountable is difficult—but easy paths don't lead to high peaks. So many people think accountability is constricting and limiting. In truth, it is the opposite; it is liberating. Furthermore, it is inspiring for others.

In my ten years as a professional basketball player, I had only one coach (yes, only one) who truly apologized in front of the whole team. He was my last coach and a true New Alpha. A short man, Juan Cardona had every right to engage in old alpha male behavior and overcompensate with a Napoleon complex, but he didn't. He came in midseason after the first coach of Fuerza Regia, the team I played for in Monterrey, Mexico, was fired. Coach Cardona immediately shifted the personnel around, cut two of my teammates, and brought in two of his own guys who he felt were a better fit. Turns out it was a horrible call. We lost six games in a row, and one of his players was a real blight on the team.

Coach Cardona finally cut his own player. After he did so, he called us together for a meeting and said, "As a man, I have to tell you I was wrong. And I am sorry. I own that. It is on me. And I will make it up to you." No buts, no excuses, no half-assed apology like saying "It's my fault—you guys weren't in good enough shape."

Nope. He gave us a genuine apology.

Do you think this made me think he was weak?

The exact opposite. I would have (and would still) run through a brick wall for that man. His humility and accountability were inspiring.

I never understood why, in every culture around the globe, so many people, especially those in leadership positions, take apologizing as a sign of weakness. Confidence and humility are two sides of the same coin, as are arrogance and insecurity. When you are confident about what you are good at, you have no problem admitting what you don't know, asking for help, or apologizing for your errors.

Asking for help is strength.

Cardona was also the coach who pulled me over to the side of a game and asked, "Lance, what are you seeing out there? What are you seeing from your perspective in the middle that I can't see from here?"

I told him what I thought, and whether he acted on my observances or not did not matter; his willingness to listen to what I had to say communicated that he valued my perspective and me as a person, and that was enough for me to trust and value his final decision. This was a big contrast with most of the coaches I played for who wouldn't even try to apologize or receive feedback and who ruled with an iron fist and a know-it-all stance to establish their authority.

The same applies to corporate, community, and political leaders who think they don't need to listen to the opinions of others. If you are dealing with this behavior from an authority figure, rest assured you are dealing with a "boss," not a leader. A boss is someone who believes taking ownership of or accountability for their faults in any kind of relationship will make them look bad and weak. Bosses rule others through fear, because their lives are ruled through fear. A boss tries to control everything. They crave and seek power, yet it eludes them, as they are unable to grasp that any power that can be taken from them is not true power.

A boss is unable to be flexible when life throws the unexpected their way. Stubbornness is their power scenario. When reality doesn't look like what the boss wants it to be, they cannot accept it and will blame others, because if they don't, in their fear-based thinking it means they weren't powerful enough.

Old alpha males believe accountability is weakness.

Know this: if you can't accept input and feedback, people will anticipate and rejoice in your failure. People want to know they are valued. If you don't let them know they have value, they will find someone else to lead them. If most bosses understood that people want to feel like they are genuinely contributing to a cause, their jobs and tenures would endure, and they would emerge as leaders.

A true leader, a New Alpha male, finds strength in building others up and leads through humility and accountability. He understands his vulnerability makes him bulletproof, for if he can truly value his authentic self, he can truly value others. By owning his shortcomings and faults, the New Alpha male has nothing to hide. He cannot be leveraged or compromised. By apologizing for any shortcoming, he leads through trust, knowing that when it is his time to step down from power, it will be the right time, for again, any power that can be taken away is not true power. A New Alpha male understands that taking accountability inspires others to strive for their own greatness.

> ## A true leader, a New Alpha male, finds strength in building others up and leads through humility and accountability.

Between social and news media, we live in a world of constant connection, yet despite the many opportunities, few people have the grit and courage to accept accountability. Most people do anything they can to avoid it, fearing that ownership of mistakes will cost them a job, a relationship, or admiration. Contrary to whatever skewed cultural affirmations tell us that people will attack us if we are flawed, accountability is inspiring. It endears people to you.

Here's an easy example: Presidents Nixon, Clinton, and Trump all made their lives much more difficult by denying and avoiding accountability when scandals arose. They kept disavowing any impropriety on their parts. In contrast, President Reagan, no matter what you think of his politics, was well loved and popular because he always jumped in front of the scandal, like during Contra-gate when he said as president, "I take full responsibility for my own actions and for those of my administration."

What happened to Reagan? His popularity only grew.

Now more than ever, people are starving for accountability in leadership. It's amazing how few of us understand that many people are quick to forgive when leaders acknowledge their shortcomings and share the lessons of humility.

So many of the leadership experiences I share have come from my own errors as a team captain and teammate, or a partner and father. I have never been perfect—not even close—but I choose to own my mistakes so I am able to learn and adapt to future scenarios rather than digging in my heels and refusing to apologize for my errors, which would never allow me to grow.

Accountability does not allow you to be anyone's victim. When you own your choices, you own your fate. When you are candid about your shortcomings, you can take true possession of your success which is made that much sweeter because you know you earned it and, more importantly, deserve it. It's those little victories, especially the ones that you reached through accountability, that keep you going through the hard times. They do for me.

Ask Yourself

» When you think of accountability, what comes to mind?
» Did you have a harsh parent, coach, or teacher who punished you for any flaw or mistake, conditioning you to believe that accountability means punishment?
» Do you avoid accountability because if you chose it you would no longer be able to play the victim/entitlement card?
» Where is your sense of accountability rooted in terms of culture, fear, projection, addiction, and the stories you tell yourself?

DEEPER ACCOUNTABILITY

If accountability has made you uncomfortable up to this point, hang on, because it's about to get worse!

The New Alpha male embraces an even deeper accountability, one that does not seek recognition because it cannot necessarily be seen from the outside. It is intrinsic. It is Alpha accountability.

Alpha accountability was first exemplified to me by my mother. The reason I have hearing loss is because I barely survived my birth in my grandmother's bedroom. Nobody in our polygamist commune took Rh incompatibility into account. My mother was a negative blood type and I was a positive, and so her body interpreted me as a parasite and tried to kill me while I was in her womb. This was a medical condition they didn't consider in our ultrareligious commune, since, after all, Jesus was coming soon. (Jesus never came.)

The second day after my birth, I grew more jaundiced, more lethargic. My mother took me out of the commune to the tiny Montana town of Hamilton, where I was saved by a medical resident from Johns Hopkins who specialized in Rh incompatibility issues because he was an Rh baby himself. After two weeks in an incubator, undergoing several complete blood changes (as opposed to transfusions), I was still alive and defying scientific explanation because my liver bilirubin titer count was well above the mortality rate. I should have been dead, and the doctor told my parents as much when he released me from the hospital, saying he didn't dare publish this in the *Journal of the American Medical Association*, because he knew no one would believe him.

There are two reasons why I am alive today:

1. On some primal level I chose to be.
2. There was and always has been someone there to help me along the way.

Accountability is knowing that it is vanity to say you arrived anywhere on your own. Accountability is owning the truth that along with your hard work and discipline there was someone there at the right time.

This doctor who saved my life was prophetic when he warned my parents to be on the watch for signs of hearing loss among other severe symptoms. When I was twenty months old, in the aftermath of the Rh factor, I was diagnosed with 80 percent hearing loss. My mother could have felt shame and guilt and blamed herself, or even been angry with the leaders in our commune who gave poor medical advice. She had every right to be the victim, but she chose accountability instead. All she could do to ameliorate her lack of awareness as a parent was to own up to her actions by having me fitted with hearing aids when I was twenty months old. There were no opportunities to learn sign language in our part of Montana, since I was the only deaf kid within fifty miles. My mother also enrolled me in speech therapy until I was fifteen. I resented my mother for years for making me go, because it was a constant reminder that I was not normal. I wanted to be normal.

Being a leader is lonely. You are never going to fit in—that is not your path.

I fought my mother every day. Every single day, I pushed back, but she never quit. She owned her part. Again, she could have laid blame onto others, but how would that have helped or empowered me to be a leader of my own life?

My mother had no immediate incentives, payoffs, or validation waiting for her. All she knew was that the buck stopped with her. She never expected a thank-you or reward.

Deeper Alpha accountability does not have standard incentives other than your own internal clarity and self-respect. Because of my mother's insistence on pushing me beyond my comfort zones, which honed my ability to adapt, I was able to function in the great wide world and am now paid for my skills as a communicator.

I didn't thank my mother until I was twenty-one years old. My gratitude was the external reward for her accountability but was never her hope or motivation—her motivation was pure, altruistic accountability.

This is Alpha.

Through my mother's example, I learned from a young age that if I wanted to live an exceptional life, I had to understand I was not an exception. The world owed me nothing. Tomorrow is promised to no one.

True Alpha accountability is a thankless endeavor. No one can validate you but you.

If I wanted to live an exceptional life, I had to first understand I was not an exception.

The New Alpha male not only holds but *seeks* accountability for his own intrinsic growth. He knows that when he does, clarity is the reward. That clarity can be lonely at times, when everyone else is not holding themselves accountable at the basic transactional level of accountability, let alone the deeper intrinsic levels. However, a true Alpha male does not need reciprocity for clarity—because clarity is an internal alchemy. The New Alpha male not only apologizes for his failures and shortcoming in a relationship or interaction but takes full accountability for the entire experience, knowing if he chooses to learn from it all, it will be for his highest good.

True Alpha male accountability calls for the most altruism one can muster.

This is hard work.

You choose to hold yourself accountable because you choose to, understanding that karma doesn't always pay us back in the same currency. True accountability is the daily act of self-reflectively checking your culture, stories, fears, addictions, and projections. It is a daily choice. I didn't hit ten free throws in a row one day and suddenly say, "Okay, I don't have to practice free throws anymore." No, it was a regular checkup, and that is accountability. Your skill of self-awareness will grow sharp through the daily routine of accountability that demands reflection and continual maintenance when it comes to identifying your stories and thought patterns.

Ask Yourself

» Do I fulfill my obligations and duties?
» Do I own my shortcomings?
» Do I honor my word?
» Do I repay my debts?
» Do I acknowledge that no one else is responsible for my happiness and reality?

Behavior of Alpha Accountability

Choose to empower yourself with the accountability of choice.

» I choose to acknowledge that everyone I encounter has something to teach me, and so I will learn from every relationship.
» I choose to identify which role I play, archetype I fulfill, or mask I wear, and which role each relationship in my life is calling forward for me to address.
» I choose to identify which habits or limiting patterns of belief are being exposed for growth through each relationship in my life.
» I choose to allow those roles and stories that are being called forward to grow beyond the childhood stage, especially if they no longer serve me.
» I choose to acknowledge that even my most painful relationships are opportunities to learn from and grow and transcend cultural roles, allowing for my true authentic self to emerge.
» I choose to face my stories.
» I choose to challenge and rewire my thought patterns that push said stories.
» I choose to confront the fears that try to rule my life.
» I choose to hold myself to deep intrinsic accountability while knowing I may never receive praise or acknowledgment—which is fine, because I do this for me.

SELF-AWARE VERSUS SELF-ABSORBED

There is a fine line between being self-absorbed and being self-aware. Self-absorbed is the limited scope and mentality where we believe everything happening around us, or even to us, is about us. A self-absorbed person asks, "Why is this happening to me? Why does this keep happening to me? What did I do to deserve this? Why do people keep betraying me? People can't be trusted. . . ." Self-absorbed people view the world through a childish lens.

In contrast, a self-aware person asks these kinds of questions:

» Why am I in this dynamic?
» What part of me was drawn to this relationship/person?
» What baggage or expectation am I projecting?
» What lesson can be attained through this experience?
» What is this person helping me learn about myself?
» What is an aspect of my personality or a blind spot I have been avoiding that is being brought to the surface to address via this experience?

A self-aware mentality keeps you on the trajectory of growth and development, of accountability, integrity, and compassion. A self-absorbed mentality keeps you in the victim mentality archetype, where growth is not found, where you live in a world of fear, scarcity, and unaccountability.

The old alpha believes enemies are all around, waiting to invade his home and bank account, to overpower and take what belongs to him. He even seeks to be offended and imposes himself into other people's projections, to make himself the center of the conflict. He holds grudges for slights and wrongdoings, because he enjoys the energy of being wronged, as he feels it entitles retribution, and thus wants to take power from another. Self-absorbed people are not reflective, as they project characteristics onto others to fit the internal narrative of their self-absorption.

The New Alpha male, through self-awareness, holds himself accountable for all the relationships and experiences in his life, knowing he can choose between being a student or a victim, even if he has been victimized. That act of choosing to be a student of life empowers him to find more clarity about who he truly is, and not who he projects others to be.

Self-aware people are reflective, knowing we can find any characteristic in another human to love or to hate. It is our choice to see those reflected characteristics and either hold a grudge (which is our own self-loathing) or hold gratitude for the mirrors and lessons revealing our true selves behind the masks we wear—that is accountability.

That is Alpha.

SPIRITUAL ACCOUNTABILITY

We have all seen people abuse the notion and concept of spirituality as a way to avoid accountability. This is ironic because spirituality without accountability is not spirituality at all. This statement might sound harsh, even dogmatic, but it is the opposite: accountability is a call, urging you to go deeper within, to own all your humanity and be empowered by self-intimacy; it is knowing your humanity is your divinity.

Spirituality is more than talking about angels and gods and prayers. It is the pursuit of emotional and mental wellness for ourselves and others, while giving ourselves permission to *feel* and understand from the heart that we are a living extension of the universe, which is conscious and alive. Alpha spirituality gets all the distractions and stories that say we are separate out of the way, so we can sync our true beating heart with the rhythm of the cosmos.

I saw people embrace my grandfather's extreme religious structure and perhaps even ignore their best judgment because they preferred the comfort of a system that enabled and fostered self-aggrandizement: *Follow the prophet and he will guide you to the highest degree of glory in heaven.* Some might say that following the rules is accountability! Not really. Following the rules at the surface level without discernment to avoid punishment or to receive merits or rewards (be it gold stars or eternal life) or to alleviate fear of the unknown is a superficial accountability. New Alpha accountability goes deeper in questioning the motive and incentive as well as analyzing the fear we are avoiding by seeking said incentives for following surface-level rules.

New Alpha accountability asks, "Do I want to know myself? *Truly?*" This is hard work. It takes us down a path where we are forced to look at all the parts of our psyche, even the "Devil" within us that we loathe so much we project him to be somewhere in the underworld, outside of us.

Many of us do not choose Alpha accountability because it can be lonely and unnerving; it can be challenging as it opens the door to *more* questions, which is the opposite of the many answers that religion and most spiritual teachers promise. I have seen many people exploited through this fear of the unknown but also given the heavy crown of guilt that said they were both sinners yet also special. What a burdensome dichotomy to bear, to avoid the gray area, the unknown.

When they sinned, or risked their eternal well-being: "I'll just repent." The get-out-of-jail-free cards pervade religious belief: repent, fast, say your prayers, tithe, . . . For me, this was never enough. It felt shallow. It felt as though people were playing mind games with themselves. I am not mocking religious rituals; I am suggesting they can be abused as soothing agents, an external alleviation of fear or guilt rather than a powerful means of internal transformation—a way to find the courage to go deeper within ourselves and ask hard questions about fear and guilt.

Simply performing an act of contrition and not working to get to the root of the offending act is like taking a painkiller to alleviate the symptom of a physical illness and not treating the real underlying cause. The same symptoms or new ones will continue to appear until you cure the disease.

If you think you might be using spirituality to bypass or create false accountability, ask yourself these questions:

> Why do I feel contrition? Because my community is disappointed in me? Or because I hurt someone else?
>
> Why was I tempted?
>
> Why am I repenting?
>
> If I hadn't been caught, would I have felt guilty?

Am I trying to find God or "oneness" or even happiness through my public acknowledgment of my sins, or am I scared of being rejected by my community if I do not?

What old stories led me down this path of self-destructive behavior?

What fear most dominates this path? Abandonment? Powerlessness?

What story am I running from or to?

What desire within me is not being met that caused me to deviate from the social order?

Does this desire/temptation promise me happiness? If so, if it clashes with my community belonging, which am I willing to lose?

What aspect of my personality is being shamed into thinking it is bad?

Do I know that story about this action being "bad" to, in fact, be true?

The trick is to ask yourself these questions from a discerning perspective and not a place of judgment. You must take off your cultural hat, observe, and allow yourself to answer. Ask these questions with self-compassion, not self-loathing or self-lionization. Allow yourself permission to grow, to transmute rather than being stuck in old stories of cultural laws and structures, believing they define you. Asking ourselves these kinds of questions and challenging our biases and preconceptions is deep Alpha accountability.

Why don't more people ask themselves these questions? Because it is uncomfortable to look in the mirror and be held accountable. When you take away the determinism excuse that says the Devil tempted you, or the martyr excuse that says God is punishing or testing you, what's left is accountability for your own actions, choices, and stories.

For me, the clarity that mental wellness and spirituality are one and the same came during the long hours in many quiet hotel rooms around the world, sitting in the dark, with no more books to read, no English television or internet access. All there was left to do was face and learn to own my physical shortcomings and failures on the basketball court and also to go deeper as I looked at the triggers, stories, and thought patterns I inherited from my extreme religious upbringing, and to see which patterns were recreating conflict in my professional and personal life.

It took the audacity to face the deep-rooted fear that was driving the vehicle of my subconscious: abandonment. I couldn't blame the Devil or a straw man anymore. I had to learn to take accountability for my reality and the stories and reactions I unleashed into said reality. To see with clarity that part of becoming an adult and a New Alpha male was to see I am the common denominator in all my experiences. To see I have been recreating and reenacting victim- or martyr-enabling situations because part of me enjoyed or had been conditioned to operate that way since I was a child as a coping mechanism to process pain and hurt. And for a while it helped, but by my mid-twenties those roles were no longer serving me in becoming an Alpha male.

I came to see that religion is following someone else's spiritual experience in hopes of belonging, while spirituality is following your own path of mental clarity and empowerment. Spirituality is the humility to be able to get yourself and your stories out of your own way. It is showing yourself to be a vessel of grace, of kindness, and of unconditional love to all around you, knowing it is not about you.

In that humility, the New Alpha male acknowledges some form of a greater intelligence—whether it be the universe, God, Great Spirit, Mother Earth, or, heck, even gravity or a central processing core. This is essential. Refusing to acknowledge a greater intelligence than ourselves is not pragmatic, as it closes us to many other experiences. We must sustain the accountability that demands humility and self-awareness to acknowledge some higher intelligence, or we will lose our footing and navigate our way through life with blinders on. Remember, confidence and humility are two sides of the same coin. And true humility is acknowledging a greater power than yourself.

I call my higher power *Creation,* for it implies I am within It, not separate from It. And it took me a while to get there because the God or Creator I was raised with was far away, which left me feeling abandoned.

In the grief following my departure from the NBA and my mental breakdown, it took me years to trust something greater than myself.

What could I even trust?

Did I believe in Earth? Could I acknowledge and pray to Mother Earth?

Yes.

Prayer and meditation are essential to our magnetic connection to energy. And that connection was reestablished with a higher power as I prepared for my first TEDx Talk, "What Is Your Polygamy?" Before I walked out onto the stage that day to speak, I prayed to Mother Earth. That was as far as I could go at the time, which is important. We must be willing to ask for help from a greater power, for when we open ourselves up, we allow magic to enter. Otherwise, we are indeed alone.

Do we get to decide what that magic will look like? No, that is your logic spinning up expectations. But we must acknowledge a higher power, so I ask you to, please, if you are not there yet, put this book down and find something to talk to. Again, if it is the earth below your feet, the stars in the sky, or the ocean, that will be enough. Acknowledging a greater intelligence allows that although you may strive and labor, you cannot accomplish great things alone. In that new, humble uncertainty, where our comfort zones once resided, is where magic and wonder can be found.

SPIRITUAL MATERIALISM

Deep Alpha accountability is not only fact-checking our stories but examining our logic and subsequent assumed truths about the nature of the vast universe itself. In the realm of quick-fix self-help books, we see a lot of coaches and influencers intertwining material wealth with spirituality. "I am so blessed," says the person with a $10 million home, insinuating in a mindless or even sinister way that God somehow loves or blessed them more because they are so deserving—compared to the hardworking schoolteacher making a modest income.

"I did 'the work' and I manifested abundance!" This is neither spirituality nor humility, but rather vanity.

"I am good at manifesting," says the person with their Bentley, trying to attract future clients to pay them money so they can make the payments on said Bentley. "All you have to do is imagine it with intention, and let the universe do the rest . . ."

This is not only *not* spirituality, it's fraud. Manifesting is hard work. It is perseverance.

I didn't make the NBA until I was twenty-seven—no fairy dust or essential oils involved.

Same went for one of my biggest inspirations: my oldest sister, Raphael. As a girl growing up in an extreme patriarchal commune, at the age of eleven she declared she wanted to be a medical doctor. People laughed and immediately tried to suppress it, saying, "Yeah, that's cute. Girls don't go to college, let alone become medical doctors."

"Watch me," she said.

Ten years later, right when our family went into hiding when we broke away from polygamy, Raphael had been accepted into medical school at the University of Utah. The following year when she saw how much I had begun to care about basketball at my new school as an eighth grader, she sat me down and said, "This is what you do: you write down your goals and you put them above your light switch, and every time you touch the light switch, on or off, you read your goals out loud. Every single time." From my sister's advice, I learned that there is great power in the spoken word and the written word. Do not underestimate this. Every goal I have written down in my life has come true in some way, shape, or form.

Did those dreams look like what I had expected or hoped them to look like?

Not always.

As a fourteen-year-old boy, I wrote up my goals and hung them over the light switch in my room. I still remember them:

I, Lance Allred, will start for my high school varsity team by my junior year.

I, Lance Allred, will average a 3.5 GPA.

I, Lance Allred, will get a college scholarship to the University of Utah.

The dreams were there.

Wishing isn't enough. Instead, when you make such a declaration, you get a download, an intuitive hit. The download that came to me when I made that first set of goals said, "I have to wake up every morning and work out with my high school coach before school for three straight years."

That was the intuition that accompanied the decree of goals. And I chased them. My parents never woke me up once over the span of three years because it was my dream, my passion. I slept with my alarm clock on my chest to wake me up early to meet my high school coach, Kerry Rupp, for an hour-long workout before the first bell.

I chased those dreams as though I was on fire.

Yet, most people give up, let alone even write down their goals, because it is hard. It's uncomfortable. It requires accountability—the accountability to do what your intuition says you have to do. It isn't so much that people don't know how much is required for them to achieve their goals, but rather that they want something easy, a shortcut.

There are no shortcuts. It takes work, despite what social media may be selling you: "Quick Success! 3 things to do to manifest your dream life NOW!"

Yes, setting goals can create expectations. Many people say they do not set goals because they want to be open to what life brings, not locked into a vision of what they want life to look like. This is a fair sentiment, but does it spur people outside of their comfort zones?

Seek balance. It is a graceful dance of setting goals and intentions and then learning to release your worth from the outcome, after you have done everything you possibly can to make those dreams come true—surrendering them to what will be.

The terms "self-development" and "wellness" have often been appropriated by commercial opportunists selling quick fixes. Many are deceiving people to value self-development as solely a means to a financial or material end. Consequently, many people give up on self-development, because their logic fails to see that the value is the transformation, not a trophy or monetary reward. Someone who says, "I have been doing this whole 'self-development' thing for more than a year and nothing financially has changed," is kidding themselves.

If you are reading this book with the sole intention of it somehow helping you make more money, get that next promotion, or be more influential, then this book is not for you. True self-development can't be bought; it is a complete restructuring from within, a transformation of your priorities and boundaries, so that you may see with clarity that those material possessions matter little in comparison to your own self-worth.

The internal reconstruction that is accountability and the subsequent transformation are uncomfortable, and most people do not want anything to do with such discomfort and will avoid it at all costs, yet they still want magic to happen. They still want a happily-ever-after. Funny thing, though: the magic that everyone seeks is outside their comfort zone. The New Alpha seeks clarity as a means in and of itself, knowing it cannot be bought, and if material possessions arrive along the way, they're just an added bonus.

This is Alpha.

Do the Work

» Write down a time when someone in your formative years showed great accountability, setting a high bar, a strong example through action.

» As you hold that thought of a mentor or role model, think about a person who you didn't show up for when they needed you—whether you broke their trust or avoided stepping up when your name was called. Over the next week, call or email one person who comes to mind.

» Take ownership of how you let them down. If you can't repair or make amends, at least let them know that you are doing your best from this point on, and to also thank them for the lesson they helped you learn about yourself.

» Apologize.

» If they do not accept your apology, that is on them and is their responsibility to work out.

» Do this every day, until it becomes a habit. There is always something we can own, something we can apologize for. We have all committed enough acts that need reconciliation. This habit will turn into a comfortable act. You will find great empowerment in your ownership of your shortcomings, with the underlying fears being brought to light as you find the courage to not commit them again in the future. That is Alpha accountability.

In the Zone: Heart Drumming and Accountability Meditation

Each meditation in this book will include heart drumming. It isn't as scary as it sounds! It's a practice that involves sitting with eyes closed and slowly thumping your chest with an open palm. Not a slap, but a thump. Do it with intent—forcefully, with strength but not harm—for at least a minute. The rhythm will become hypnotic and help you turn off your conscious mind as your brain rests in a Theta brainwave state—almost like deep sleep—that opens us to learning, meditation, and insight.

So many of us mistake meditation as something that happens outside of our body, but that's not the case. Pounding on your chest will force you to be in your body. This may be uncomfortable as you pound stress out of your body, and your pectoral muscle may grow sore. Respect that and remember we are not doing this with rage but with humility.

This heart drumming will center you with presence in your heart space, a place where many men do not dare to go, not just figuratively but literally, as they attempt to shield it with bench presses and over-developed pectoral muscles.

» For this meditation practice, write the word *accountability*. Focus on the word in your mind. Notice what you feel, not what you think. What notions have you had about it? Are they still prevalent? Do they induce fear?

» Now begin heart drumming.

» As your body relaxes and becomes centered, the rhythmic drumming will quiet your brain. When you feel that your conscious brain and its worries have stilled, stop drumming.

» Take a deep breath. Focus on the breath coming into your opened heart space. Notice how it feels after you have drummed all the stress out of it.

» In that open space, allow accountability to take a new form within and around you. What shape does it begin to manifest itself into? A human? A statue? An animal? Allow it to become more than an idea, as everything is energy.

» Take notes; write down how it is appearing in your deep state of mind.

» If you have had a negative feeling toward accountability and all the consequences that you see in our society toward those who screw up, ask accountability, as an entity in and of itself, to show you something different. Listen to what it has to say, what it wants you to feel.

» Allow accountability to dwell in your heart space, giving you courage where stress and fear once resided.

RECAP

Accountability is inspiring for those around you, knowing it is a safe space to recognize faults, blind spots, and shortcomings. When we take full ownership of our flaws, we can take true credit for our victories—and those victories are that much more rewarding. Accountability is not punishment; it is empowerment. It is leadership. Deep Alpha accountability positions us to transcend superficial habits that are merely distractions and go inward to integrity.

4

INTEGRITY

The Second Principle of Perseverance

IN THE AFTERMATH OF THE GAME, I sit quietly, choosing not to put my hearing aids in as the coach storms back and forth, cussing and spewing rage following the team's loss. I could make eye contact, but I choose not to because I can't look the coach in the eye—not because I let him down, but because I do not respect him.

He is the coach who only shows his true and ugly self when the TV cameras are not around—behind closed doors in the locker room when nobody but the team is watching. He is never the same person in every room he walks into. In this space, he exudes fear—prevalent and palpable, reeking of insecurity, which lets us know he will throw any of us under the bus at any moment to save his own skin.

As with so many people in positions of power, fear has rotted away his integrity.

The coaches I enjoyed most weren't necessarily the nice coaches, but the consistent ones—the coaches who never changed their personality, whether the cameras were on or if the owner was in the room. These were the coaches I knew would always have our backs. If they were firm with one player, they were firm with every player.

There were no double standards. Double standards are the quickest way to destroy your team. They are the result of absent integrity.

The coach who didn't tolerate double standards and who treated everyone the same was the coach who valued his own integrity, and thus his players' dignity. This was leadership. Say what you will about Bobby Knight, the legendary, albeit grumpy, coach most famously from the University of Indiana. But he was grumpy on camera and he was grumpy off camera. There is integrity in that.

Integrity is my favorite of the Seven Principles of Perseverance because theoretically it should be the easiest, but in fact it is one of the most difficult.

DEFINING INTEGRITY

Integrity is the daily choice to remain consistent in who you are, no matter who is watching, despite the never-ending temptations of immediate short-term gain. Merriam-Webster defines it as "the state of being whole and undivided," and that's how I see integrity—embodying all aspects of who you are.

The New Alpha is the same person in every room he enters.

Here's a promise I'll make to anyone: If you remain true to who you are, never compromising yourself for the short-term gain, you will get to where you need to go. Maybe not to where you want to go, but where you need to go.

Sometimes my integrity was all I had, especially on many dark and cold winter mornings during basketball season. Often I got out of bed unsure of where my path was taking me, but I always knew if I stayed true to who I was, I would get to where I needed to go, and that small glimmer was sometimes all I had to get me to lace up my shoes one more time and get back to work. When you function from a place of integrity, you cannot fail.

This is Alpha.

LIVING INTEGRITY

My mother and father were my first living example of integrity, when as Allreds, they treated everyone exactly the same in our polygamist commune. This made my parents an anomaly, for being Allreds, we were royalty within the polygamist group known as the "Allred group," though technically called the AUB, or Apostolic United Brethren. You would think that within a theoretically socialist community, equality would be a given, but this was not the case. In fact, it was hierarchal and rife with nepotism. Even so, my parents made no distinction, and no matter what their last name was, treated everyone the same, and that is why they were loved by many and consequently a threat to other men in power in the commune.

Because of this dynamic, we ended up leaving Montana to move to Utah, into the main headquarters of the Allred group, as the Montana commune was just a hub. My father became the right-hand man to his uncle, Owen, who was our religious leader at the time. Eventually, when I was twelve years old, my father blew the whistle on child abuse and money laundering by the entire AUB group. His conscience would not allow himself to function in a world of double standards and hypocrisy that are so often prevalent when power is abused. His integrity and consistency of character were more important to him than personal gain.

Faced with a choice, my father chose truth and integrity, knowing it might well cost everything he had worked his entire life for. All the homes he had built for free in the communes, all the work he had put in as the scholar and theologian for the Allred group to continue his father's legacy, were gone. At forty-two years of age, he and my mother were forced to cut their losses, leave everything behind, and go into hiding.

They lost all they had; that was the price of integrity.

I know they would pay that price again without batting an eye. My parents taught me through their actions how I define integrity as an adult, which is through a question I ask myself every night when I go to bed: *Was I the same person in every room I walked into?*

People follow leaders who act with integrity because they know what they are going to get every day in that consistency of character. Are you the same person to everyone, in every room you walk into? It's not that hard: if you are behaving in a way that would be embarrassing if your mother saw it or if captured on video, then you probably shouldn't behave that way. Pretty easy criteria to follow.

I am an introvert, compounded by my hearing loss, and at large gatherings I will stand in a corner and watch the room. I will notice many people change their body language and posture depending on who they are talking to, even outright changing their personalities. It never ceases to amaze me how many people do this, especially those in leadership positions, and more alarming is how they fail to process that other people might notice this behavior.

The lack of self-awareness is stunning.

If I watch someone change their personality depending on who is in the room, I know I cannot do business with that person. Their chameleon traits signal clearly they will throw me under the bus once they are able to make a move for their own immediate benefit. Outdated alpha males are chameleons. They will cheat or compromise themselves to get ahead. They will throw people under the bus to protect themselves and their own agenda and motives and climb the corporate ladders of their workplaces to receive validation. They will be who they have to be in any room, to serve their ultimate agenda: their own personal gain. And their superficial success will paint the illusion of happiness.

The old alpha will appear successful and happy to the world as he ascends to the top, but be clear in understanding that most of the people who cut corners and use others for their own gain will have burned so many bridges along the way that they will have no intimate relationships with whom to share their victory. And even more starkly, they don't even know who they are anymore. In the absence of intimacy, the hole within their heart grows bigger, making them more restless in their search for a new goal, accomplishment, or trophy to temporarily validate them, believing that external validation will give them connection.

Ask Yourself

» Are you the same person no matter who is in the room, whether they have money or influence or power, or not? Do you treat everyone the same?

» Recall a time when an authority figure's behavior (a parent, church leader/teacher, or a boss) was inconsistent. Did that seem acceptable? Did this experience affirm how the "game of life" had to be played? Or did you have the skill of personal reflection and realize you didn't have to play by those rules?

» Think of a time when you were in a quandary and you gave in to peer pressure or acted selfishly versus keeping your integrity intact. Recall a time where you chose the immediate, easy, and superficial gain. (Don't worry, we've all done it!) Then recall a time where despite immense temptation, you chose integrity. Write down a list of the feelings you felt in both instances. Be honest! There will be good and bad emotions on both lists—otherwise, we would always choose the high road.

GOOD GUY VERSUS NICE GUY

There is a difference between a nice guy and a good guy, which author Robert Glover so brilliantly pointed out. For a long time, I thought being a nice guy would get me where I wanted to be in life. It didn't. In fact, it left me with little in both relationships and finances, a basement apartment, and overwhelming credit card debt. It wasn't until I learned how to be a good guy that my life started to flow with more ease and abundance.

When I began playing basketball as a teen, I underwent a personality schism. Everyone loved seeing cutthroat "Dark" Lance on the basketball court, but that Lance was not allowed inside the family home. I had to be nice "Light" Lance when I was with my family. I began to live a compartmentalized life—Dark Lance on the court, Light Lance off the court. I deluded myself into thinking that was integrity, because I was still the same person in those respective paradigms. It wasn't until after I retired from basketball that I realized how essential Dark Lance was to my well-being—this was my shadow side, the aspect of my personality that many would publicly shame but secretly admire. My shadow side carried me through a lot of hard times. It gave me the will to get back up time and again when I got blindsided by a screen I couldn't hear coming, or when a coach threw me under the bus. My need to win or just even the score, which was shamed off the court for being too aggressive, carried me through so much. It was and still is a huge part of who I am.

The trick is learning to balance dark and light.

Being exclusively nice or aggressive is not natural. Earth is always half in daylight, half in darkness. Total darkness or light would mean the end for the inhabitants of our planet. The Earth needs a balance of both to keep its equilibrium. It's the same for people—when we are shamed by religion or culture to be light all the time, it's a power play to keep us off balance.

My culture taught me that being a nice guy leads to a reward from God. I was always trying to be the nice guy, in hopes people would give me what I wanted without communicating, which was usually just to not be abandoned. I was afraid of anyone being upset with me until I was on the basketball court; then I didn't care. The mask was on. I went for blood. The dark came out. In the gladiator arena this was acceptable, for the mask provides us anonymity even from ourselves.

When I retired from basketball, I no longer had the familiar outlet of basketball to let my dark side come out. I was not in integrity, and I believe this contributed to my battles with depression and scrupulosity. Rage built, because I was not fully integrated into my personality, and thus, I was not truly functioning in integrity.

Integrity is the integration of all aspects of your personality.

It was during an issue with my son's mother following our split that a point came when I was either going to let my boundaries be undermined or I was going to have to let Dark Lance, the Lance that everyone cheered on the basketball court, emerge and integrate with me in the real world. Dark Lance came out and began setting pretty strict boundaries, much to the chagrin of people who were used to Nice Lance.

How dare Dark Lance step beyond the basketball court!

Tough. They would have to deal with it.

My dark side is a huge part of me and what makes me, me. To keep it hidden only creates a Dr. Jekyll and Mr. Hyde dynamic of mental unwellness: anxiety, depression, and other afflictions. I'm not alone—your dark side will emerge, basketball court or not, and to deny it will only make things worse.

I am not saying it is okay to lash out and be an angry male, ranting and raving on social media, vomiting hate speech and misogyny, getting into bar fights, and kicking kittens. I am speaking the opposite: the men who behave that way are angry men who have not learned to integrate their dark and light sides. They are off-balance and are thus acting in extremes.

The more you integrate and honor your dark and your light, the less extreme your outbursts will be and the fewer soothing addictions and vices you'll seek. When we hide parts of ourselves and they become shadowed, they grow stronger until they find an outlet, usually in reaction or defect. The skillful integration of both dark and light into your personality means speaking your feelings clearly without apologizing. It is stating your boundaries succinctly, and not needing to explain them. It is letting someone know if they breach those boundaries. It is treating others as you want to be treated, and if someone doesn't honor you in kind, releasing them from the relationship.

Good guys integrate all aspects of their personality, dark and light, and aren't apologetic about it. A nice guy hides aspects of his personality, hoping he can manipulate others into not judging him and thus give him what he wants. I perpetuated this pattern in professional and personal settings. Imagine my rage when the coaches always acquiesced to the difficult teammates, the "assholes." This created a culture of double standards within our team, and we know there is no quicker way to kill a team than double standards. In secret, I always envied those teammates for having the courage and sense of self to not care if someone thought they were an asshole. But in my self-righteous public persona, I judged them for not being "team-first." And while there was truth that they were not as team oriented as I, there is also truth that I was too scared of abandonment, of losing my job, and thus I always played the nice guy.

Nice guys are the most dishonest people. And I was one of them, as I was not functioning in honest integrity in my relationships—I never truly said what I wanted or what I was truly thinking and feeling. I kept quiet, hoping that my niceness would get me what I wanted, that I could somehow manipulate and hope others would read my mind and then magically give me what I wanted without me having to articulate it.

This is not integrity. It is manipulation and dishonesty, not to mention seeing the world through a childish lens. I am guilty of it. Sure, I was the same person in every room I walked into, except the basketball court. In all other rooms, I was the nice guy. Thus, my own dislike of the coaches who did not function in integrity was my own projected self-loathing and fear.

I was not integrated.

Even in my short-lived marriage, I was the nice guy. I was terrified to say no, for fear that my partner would be upset with me. What I evoked instead was her irritation that she could never connect. Can you imagine how frustrating it would be to be married to me in that context? I never truly said how I felt: I would not say no even when it was appropriate. Without clear communication and boundaries, all we had was escalating frustration. If I had said my truth instead of holding it in for fear of abandonment, she and I both would have been happier. The more we are unable to say no, the more people lose respect for us. I didn't understand for many years that what I truly wanted to be (and what the women I dated wanted) was a good guy, not a nice guy.

The New Alpha male is a good guy, not a nice guy. He speaks authentically and lives with integrity, knowing that even if his boss or partner is angry with him for saying no, he will still be respected for speaking his authentic feelings and drawing his boundaries. If people abandon him, not appreciating his authentic self and voice, the New Alpha male knows that as he integrates all aspects of who he is, the right people will integrate with him.

True integrity is the acknowledging, honoring, and integrating of all aspects of yourself.

THE GREEKS AND AVATAR DECODING

One day when I was in Greece, having a coffee before practice, I sat outside a shop in front of the Acropolis and began to have a conversation with a local. I asked him, "What does a boy growing up in Greece think about the pantheon and the gods of Olympus? Of Zeus and Hera, Poseidon and Demeter, Athena and Apollo, and the rest?"

His reply was so simple: "We are the same characters."

In that one sentence, he spoke a thousand truths about the human psyche.

With my hearing loss, I have always been a keen observer of the human body and its communication patterns. I can answer questions without fully hearing them, because I know the third or fourth question a stranger is going to ask me. I count the syllables and know they are usually asking either "Where did you play basketball?" or "Where are you from?"

I have become so sensitive to patterns that when the Greek man answered "We are but the same characters," you can imagine my elation.

I knew I was in fact not crazy to feel I was in the movie *The Truman Show*—a simulation of characters and archetypes.

As I explored my own blind spots, wanting to improve my weaknesses and be harder to guard not just as a basketball player but as a human being, I was first drawn to Myers-Briggs and Enneagram testing, which are quite interesting as personality traits tests. Then I began to look at and decode my own astrological chart, learning the foundational language that I began blending with my own experiences and intuition into what I now call "avatar decoding."

This is not to be confused with the kind of magical-thinking astrology where the superstitious blame Mercury retrograde from a lack of understanding, or nervously check horoscopes, believing their sun sign, which is merely one aspect of them, can predict an entire future identical to the other hundreds of millions of people who share that sign. Rather, astrology-based avatar decoding, as I tell my clients, is a mirror of self-awareness. It has dozens of different aspects other than sun signs that help us see where all the persona archetypes of this matrix, encapsulated in the Greek pantheon, have been encoded in you from the gravitational-powered cipher, or software coder, that is our solar system.

Here's where some of you are probably saying, "Lance has lost his mind."

Possibly, but think about the moon. We feel and acknowledge its cycles, affecting the oceans' tides and likely women's cycles. Furthermore, most doctors say that the ER is craziest during a full moon. As we all collectively agree to this truth of the gravitational pull of the moon and consider its effects on our subconscious, would it not stand to reason that Jupiter, which is eleven times the diameter of Earth and nearly eighty-eight times the diameter of the moon, would also have some gravitational pull and effect on our planet and, thus, our psyches? It may not be as immediate as Earth's moon or as intense, but nevertheless, isn't that gravity and the power of its orbit real? Well then, what about all the other planets?

When the ancient Greeks looked to the stars and began to tell the myths associated with them in the form of the Gods of their pantheon, it wasn't that they believed those stories to be factual history but that they were metaphors of the human psyche. In short, astrology was an early form of Myers-Briggs personality classifications, where personalities were decoded to show their strengths and weaknesses.

Mapping and tracking the planets and stars, coinciding their angles with when people were born, the Greeks began to decipher human psychology, recognizing we all have archetypes or universal patterns within our collective unconscious. This connects to the theories of nineteenth-century Swiss psychiatrist and psychoanalyst Carl Jung, who described the "unified self" as comprised of parent, child, a trickster archetype, and other elements. What Jung's work introduced to the modern world was that we all wear many masks or personae that comprise our larger psyche, with different characters or personas having larger influence or sway. The Greeks were doing the same thing in interpreting people's psyches according to their astrological charts.

Decoding the masks or avatars of my psyche on a chart, I began to see my patterns and blind spots. My time stamp, my code that is a birth chart, as I deciphered it, explained so much. This applies to all of us—our code is the avatar of how we are naturally programmed to react to the world in this vibrational dimension. That time stamp is part of our software, which integrates with our cultural upbringing.

Explore—allow reason to merge with wonder, integrating your mind with your heart.

Our task is to transcend that code and learn to respond to the world with clarity rather than reacting from the old stories and prejudices of our culture and natural temperament that are revealed in our code. There is always free will and choice—agency to make the decision to continue through life on autopilot, which is our astrological code, or the decision to transcend that code, which is Alpha.

Simply being aware of our coding, our strengths, and more importantly, our weaknesses and blind spots, is half the battle. Once we accept that, we see our ego—or what I see as our autopilot, our avatar: how we react to the world when we are not self-aware. Most of us go through life asleep, unaware of the machine and software code of our mind running on the predictable behaviors and dynamics of the planets and archetypes that were ciphered in our avatar when we were born into this matrix.

If you haven't noticed it yet, the solar system looks a lot like an atom, right?

Which only begs the question of scale.

Is our solar system merely an atom within a molecule that is a synapse within the brain cell of another being of a different scale and dimension? If you have looked at images of galaxies clustering and connecting, they begin to take the shape and pattern of something that looks quite similar to the synapses firing within a human brain.

Everything is energy and frequency. And we as a species have fooled ourselves into thinking our vibrational frequency as humans is the only frequency other life-forms and consciousness can exist within, rather than maybe asking with humility, "Are we merely vibrating at a frequency that is this dimension, which is within the brain of another being? And are there other galaxies and worlds, vibrating at fractal frequencies at smaller scale, within our own hands?"

This is an exploration of the concept of scale.

There is nothing wrong with allowing your brain to go there, to marvel at how insignificant we might be. It is liberating. In that space of no boundaries, no absolute truths, we see how magical this universe is, knowing that a simple name for it, such as "universe," can never truly explain it.

If you want to find magic again in this linear, left-brained, hypermasculine world of dry statistical logic, allow your mind to stay and play with the concept of scale and frequency. Allow your mind to understand that just because our human senses can only process certain frequencies doesn't mean that there can't be a million other frequencies vibrating from within this universe, let alone the parallel and perpendicular universes. Explore—allow reason to merge with wonder, integrating your mind with your heart.

AWARENESS OF LIMITATIONS AND DIS-INTEGRITY

Integrity is an act of accountability that is the full integration of all aspects of your psyche, masculine and feminine, or dark and light—seeing and decoding yourself, in full reflection and awareness. Disintegration is the opposite.

I do not care how you do it—astrology in the dark and light interpretations of your psyche, Enneagram testing or Myers-Briggs personality evaluations online, or workbooks like the CliftonStrengths Assessment—but find a healthy modality to map and expose your blind spots. Going through life without the self-awareness of seeing your own reactive patterns and blind spots is the equivalent of a basketball player never watching himself on film to see where he is weakest and can improve. If a basketball player does not take the time to see and acknowledge his limitations, that lack of self-awareness will leave him exposed to be exploited by his opponents, who no doubt found his weakness while scouting him.

The all-time greats developed new skills during every off-season, making themselves harder to guard in the upcoming season. I was by no means the most talented—if you had asked most professional scouts if Lance Allred was going to have a ten-year professional career, they would have laughed. Yet, my awareness of my own limitations and weaknesses as a basketball player became a strength because it gave me the drive to improve during each off-season as I developed and honed new skills, making me more cerebral and more difficult to guard. It allowed me to outlast so many other players.

Finding and acknowledging my weaknesses as a basketball player allowed me to hedge weak points and protect my flank by developing other skills to cope and adjust. The same thing is required of us as we play the game of life. If we do not take the time to develop the self-awareness of our strengths, weaknesses, and blind spots, we will continually be blindsided and incredibly easy to guard. So find a method to help acknowledge and honor all parts of your psyche, even the weak points that you have been taught to shame, even the dark parts. When this dark or shadow side is acknowledged and not repressed, a healthy balance of moderation will result, as well as an integration of your psyche, allowing you to no longer hide behind the avatar mask you were conditioned and coded to wear.

Integration is integrity.

This is Alpha.

THE COST OF INTEGRITY

In the summer of 1998, the year the University of Utah lost to Kentucky in the national championship game, I was offered a scholarship to the University of Utah by Coach Rick Majerus. I was seventeen years old. My dreams had come true, just like I had written them on my goal sheet.

At first, my relationship with Coach Majerus was a perfect fit. He was a brilliant "x and o" tactician and brutal taskmaster who demanded hard work. I was his archetypal player because my work ethic was intense for many reasons, but mostly fear. Fear that if I didn't become the first deaf player in NBA history, I would be a failure. Even after my family broke away from polygamy, deeply embedded in my subconscious was the *story* that God was angry with me. I put tremendous pressure on myself as I lay in bed after every game and every practice perseverating over all the mistakes I made on the court. I truly believed that every made or missed shot had eternal ramifications.

I could never do enough, such was my fear, and for a coach like Majerus, it was a perfect fit. I adored him. At his basketball camps as a teenager, I watched him command such attention, knowledge, and detail. I watched him analyze basketball games on national television with such charisma. I hung on Coach Majerus's every word and would have done anything for him. I couldn't see how dangerous this was, as are all stories when there is an imbalance of power.

My freshman year, Coach Majerus took a leave of absence when his mother was diagnosed with cancer. When he returned, something had changed. He had been demanding before, but his criticism shifted from constructive to personal. I have great compassion for the situation—dealing with cancer in regard to a loved one is enough to make anyone break—yet even before then, I had begun to see that Coach Majerus was a different person in private in the team room than he was on camera. Are you the same person in every room that you walk into?

During my sophomore year it all came crashing down. It was a pre-game shootaround, and Coach Majerus had us lined up on the baseline and began to cuss us out. Then he looked at me and said, "Lance, you are the worst of all. You use your hearing as an excuse to weasel your way through life and are a disgrace to cripples. If I was in a wheelchair and saw you play basketball, I would shoot myself."

Are you the same person in every room that you walk into?

Now, as a thirty-eight-year-old man, if someone said that to me, I would nod my head and say, "Thank you for your feedback," and then compassionately suggest they seek help for their anger. But when you are a twenty-year-old athlete with big dreams and a fragile sense of self, it breaks you. When you are trained to be a gladiator, people don't care about your feelings. You aren't supposed to have them.

I tried my best to swallow this remark and ignore it, but such abuse from a mentor turns one into a zombie. I was afraid to even play basketball anymore. I felt I had failed. Every further mistake was one more confirmation that I was a horrible person and that God and everyone else wanted nothing to do with me.

I transferred out of the University of Utah after that sophomore season was over, ready to quit basketball. I only got one scholarship offer—Weber State University.

The head coach, Joe Cravens, had at one point been an assistant under Majerus and knew what went on behind closed doors. When I transferred to Weber State, I was diagnosed with post-traumatic stress disorder (PTSD) and obsessive-compulsive disorder (OCD), which began to creep into my schoolwork and dating and inability to sleep. The PTSD was only made worse as I had to sit out that season as a "red shirt," unable to play due to NCAA transfer rules and thus unable to channel my neuroses onto the court.

I was not easy to deal with, yet Coach Cravens offered me only patience and compassion. I will always love him for it. I remember the day I walked into Coach Cravens's office and, with so much shame, told him I had been diagnosed with mental illness. He looked at me and said, "Lance, you needing to take medication for your PTSD is the same as your teammate Brad needing to take insulin for his diabetes."

This compassion meant the world to me.

Where Majerus used intimidation, threats, and fear to motivate his players, Cravens relied more on loyalty and compassion. If Majerus had understood that loyalty and compassion were the greatest motivators, not fear and intimidation, he would have been one of the top five coaches in the history of basketball. He was that brilliant.

My junior year, Majerus and the Utes came up to Weber State. We lost, but I played well. Well enough that people were asking, "Lance Allred doesn't suck. What is going on?"

Then the stories about what happened during my time at the University of Utah grew.

The Salt Lake Tribune interviewed me. And I finally told my story after two years of silence.

Why?

Two reasons—the first two of the Seven Principles of Perseverance:

> » Accountability: It was time to own up for all the times I
>   was a Ute and helped the coaches recruit other players by
>   keeping silent.
> » Integrity: Could I be the same person in every room I
>   walked into?

I was now faced with a predicament similar to what my parents faced when they blew the whistle on child abuse in the Allred group. It took a moment like this, to see how brave and bold my parents were, knowing they would not only likely be losing their family and community and everything they had worked so hard for in the chasing of their dream of a utopian society, but they would be hated, loathed with fury.

Yet, if I was able to witness my parents do the right thing, with integrity, in the face of such potential loss, how could I claim to be their son and not do the right thing by telling the truth?

The price they paid would have been for nothing if I didn't speak truth.

Furthermore, having been in speech therapy for sixteen years, learning how to speak and communicate is the thing I am most grateful for. If I didn't speak truth, then it would have all been for naught.

I shared the truth with the newspaper. The account was confirmed by teammates. A week after it was published, Coach Majerus resigned.

This was 2004.

I knew the backlash would come.

I had broken the unspoken agreement that is the code of silence demanded in sports locker rooms, but codes of silence don't mean much to me after having escaped polygamy. It means something is going on that people don't want others to know about—which is an assault on integrity.

Upon being called up to the NBA four years later, I was sitting with a scout one day, and he said, "Majerus threw quite a cloud over you. Even without the hearing loss, it is a miracle you made it here." To this day, I still get random hate messages from Utah fans. I have been called every name in the book. People will hold onto their stories about what they believe to be true. As Mark Twain said best, "How easy it is to make people believe a lie, and [how] hard it is to undo that work!"

Even when you calmly ask a screaming Majerus fan who is literally in your face, "If what I had said was untrue, why wasn't I or the *Salt Lake Tribune* sued for slander?" They do not want to hear it. Over time I have been able to give them compassion and understanding. Life is hard. It is unfair. Yet, sport is one thing that takes away that anxiety and pain for a moment. A father can take his boy to a sporting event, spending their hard-earned money to share a moment. To ride with their underdog Runnin' Utes—all the way to the national championship game—only to come so close.

That is a sacred memory. Rightfully so. And that memory should hold for them. No matter what happened with Majerus following that magical run, that memory is not cheapened. It was magic. I watched it from my TV—I was there, too.

Both truths can exist, without one negating the other. Coach Majerus was a brilliant coach who did love his players in his own way, *and* he unraveled after his mother got cancer. And with compassion, I understand that most of those fans, short for fanatics, have a fear that their magical memories of those Runnin' Ute games will mean less if both truths exist. And for some, those memories are truly highlights of their lives. Life can be hard, so we hold onto the magical stories when we can.

Those magical memories do not become invalid or lessen in some way if both truths exist. We can allow the dark and light truths of life to hold the balance of this earthly experience. For it is the human condition.

If Coach Majerus were still alive today and I saw him again, I would give him a hug and tell him, "Thank you for showing me the path of integrity I needed to take."

The old alpha would want revenge, whereas the New Alpha male understands that so many of us are operating from fear. How much fear must Coach Majerus have been in to live such a polarized life of charm and rage? Who would envy that? I wish him peace, wherever he may be, with gratitude for not only showing me the price we pay for our integrity, but also helping me understand the price my parents paid when they risked everything to stand up for truth and integrity.

This is compassion.

Do the Work

Integrity is assimilating and being accountable for all of the aspects of yourself.

» Find and take a Myers-Briggs or Enneagram personality test online or check out the CliftonStrengths Assessment books published by Gallup or *Sacred Contracts* by Caroline Myss and begin to analyze your reflection in the world and how it reflects back on you.
» Begin to study and honestly write down your strengths and weaknesses not only as a professional, but as a husband, son, brother, and father.
» For every weakness, write down a correlating strength. Compliment yourself for your strength, and do not judge yourself for your weakness.

- » Once you have the list, put it someplace visible, so you can keep your strengths and weaknesses fresh and in the forefront of your mind. Look at it every day with self-awareness so you can check your default mechanisms, catching yourself when you want to wear a different mask out of fear someone will judge, punish, or abandon you.
- » Every day will get easier, and you will become not only more confident and inclusive of all aspects of yourself but more appreciative as well. Your weaknesses will show you wonderful opportunities to grow and integrate, rather than keeping them shadowed.
- » Find a small stone or some tiny object that can serve as a token or reminder that you keep in your pocket. Every time you touch it, remember to be the same person in every room you walk into, in full trust that the right people who will value you for you will appear and help you on your path in life. Understand that the people who would only help you if they thought you were somebody else are not your tribe.

In the Zone

- » Sit erect on the ground, cross-legged or legs straight. After you have closed your eyes and taken a few deep breaths and allowed your thoughts to calm, begin heart drumming.
- » When you feel the Theta state of relaxation and heart-centeredness, take seven deep breaths, counting inward to seven, holding it for seven seconds, and then exhaling slowly for seven seconds.
- » During each set imagine one of the seven colors of the rainbow, starting from the bottom—holding red for seven seconds, then orange, yellow, green, blue, indigo, and violet.
- » Once you have settled into a deep state, allow all seven colors to reflect a part of your personality. Does red represent your temper? What does orange represent? Your sexuality? How about yellow? What comes to mind? Your confidence, or is it your shyness? I won't answer for you. This is you exploring all the many dimensions that make you, you.

» After you have worked with all seven colors, take one more breath and hold it for thirty seconds. In that time, imagine all of the colors merging into a blinding white. As you hold your breath, counting to thirty, the back of your eyelids will begin to flash white.

» Allow the white in the back of your eyelids to materialize the white in your mind, integrating all aspects of your personality.

» As you close, ask for the courage and support to remain in integrity, all aspects of you integrated throughout the rest of the day, with no colors splintering off.

RECAP

Integrity is consistency of character, full transparent ownership, and integration of all parts of your psyche—always being the same person in every room you walk into. It is not only reassuring for those around you when you are consistent, it is reassuring for yourself, knowing that you have never compromised who you are, and that staying true to yourself will take you where you need to be in life. As you integrate all aspects of who you are, the right people will integrate with you.

COMPASSION

The Third Principle of Perseverance

I FEEL SO EXPOSED and vulnerable when they rip my hearing aids out.

I try to grab them back, but I am bigger and clumsier as they toss my hearing aids back and forth between them. I can't really hear what they are saying, but I know they are exaggerating the vocal articulations of those with deafness and hearing loss.

In that moment, instead of crying or walking away, I simply stare at these other two kids who are a grade older than I am, as a thought enters my mind: *What is going on in their lives that is so bad they want to come after me to make me feel worthless? What is their homelife like that they would have to take it out on me: maybe their dad abuses them; maybe their parents ignore them?*

I don't know the answers, but I try to understand. Unpredictably to me at the time, the kids soon grew bored and tossed my hearing aids into the bushes and walked away, never to bother me again. I discovered in that moment that compassion—putting yourself in another's shoes—protects you. Compassion is the third of the Seven Principles of Perseverance and is arguably the most difficult one to practice every day.

DEFINING COMPASSION

Although I don't hear well, I have learned to listen, and listening with compassion is far more effective than being the smartest guy in the room—not only in regard to leadership ability, but in finding intimacy and finding what I am seeking.

This is Alpha.

People mistakenly assume compassion makes us a doormat. It does not—quite the opposite. Compassion gets you outside of your head, not allowing you to internalize or personalize the attacks of others. It leads to the clarity of one of the fundamental truths I have learned from my travels around the world: *People inflict pain because they are in pain.*

Projection.

We realize that when people hurt or betray us, it isn't really about us. Compassion forces us out of the self-absorbed victim vantage point of a childhood lens to the adult lens of self-awareness, which is seeing we are not the center of the universe and thus don't need to embed ourselves into other people's drama and painful stories.

Empathy and compassion do not allow us to hold grudges, and that is one of the kindest things we can do for ourselves, as grudges keep us stuck in a story where our energy grows stagnant, unable to adapt. And if we cannot adapt, let alone move, we have lost the game.

COMPASSIONATE BOUNDARIES

Checking our compassion allows us to see that when others are falling short of accountability and integrity, they are doing so from a place of fear. Fear of not being enough, which they believe leads to powerlessness or abandonment. Why judge someone who lives in fear? What a horrible place to be.

This is not to say we should enable and allow hurtful and irresponsible behavior. Rather, we do the opposite with compassion. It is caring to hold others accountable and call out their behavior and lack of integrity, but we can do so with compassionate boundaries, not reaction. By "compassionate boundaries" I mean the ability to hold space for others, while at the same time not letting them suck all your energy.

Emotionally unwell or unhappy people don't want compassion; they want our drama. Yet holding such people accountable while maintaining compassionate boundaries is in fact one of the greatest acts of unconditional love we can show. If we do not hold people accountable, we are not allowing them to see their behavior reflected back to them, as all relationships are potential mirrors to help us learn about ourselves.

The boundaries of the New Alpha are compassionate boundaries that are set from a place of clarity. Many people think to hold a boundary is to return someone's assault or attack of energy with an equal or greater amount of vitriol and hurt. "I punched him because he punched me first." This is not setting boundaries, but rather a reaction.

> ## The boundaries of the New Alpha are compassionate boundaries that are set from a place of clarity.

The old alpha male demands an eye for an eye. He insists on respect and repercussions for any slight against his boundaries, fearing if he doesn't react, others will see it as weakness.

Whereas the New Alpha male does not feel any need to save face, knowing such stories serve only the insecure. He is an alchemist, who understands that energy cannot be destroyed, only converted, as he transmutes the emotionally transmitted diseases like fear and insecurity from others into positive energy and sends it back out into the world, holding firm in his boundaries that he does not need to hold any energy that does not serve him.

When people are wishing to do you harm, compassion gives you a clearer mind to see where they are weakest in their fear. You can dismantle your enemy in defense of your boundaries and still love them and grieve for them in their fear, like you would a frightened and wounded wild beast lashing out in pain.

This is Alpha.

COMPASSION AS INTIMACY

In a world that is trying to find all the data to inoculate itself to avoid heartbreak and disappointment, we have lost sight of the truth that a broken heart is one of the most valuable things we can possess, for it opens us up to learn true compassion and empathy for others.

Most importantly, a broken heart leads to compassion for ourselves.

Compassion is the act of unconditional love that is seeing others for who they truly are, behind the archetypes and roles they play—seeing them as the spiritual beings and stardust of the cosmos that we all are.

Compassion is intimacy.

It is seeing ourselves—even our soul self—behind all the masks we were taught to wear to belong, understanding that we are already part of the universe. Everything is energy, and we are all connected, even if we can't see it through the limited processing machine that is our brain.

Holding compassion for ourselves allows us to deconstruct all the tribal narratives that say we are separate, not only from others and Creation but also from our own heart. Seeing with clarity that we are part of the universe and can never be separated is intimacy.

Over the years I have had many coaches betray me and throw me under the bus out of fear for their jobs. They made me the scapegoat to buy themselves a little more credit or time. Yet every coach who fired me during the season ended up losing his job later that same season. I say this not with spiteful vindication, but rather confirmation of the world of fear they operated under that created a self-fulfilling prophecy. They were so obsessed and afraid of losing their jobs that in their madness they made choices that only manifested their fear.

Rather than hating these coaches and letting their illness of fear contaminate me, I choose to give them compassion, knowing their world of fear is already hell enough. I see these coaches with compassion and even gratitude for the mirrors they held that reflected my own fear and internal stories. And there is intimacy in that compassion.

Choose to get out of your own head when people project their painful stories at you. With accountability, don't allow yourself to make it about you, and you will be surprised at how easy it is to continue to pick yourself up when people hurt or betray you—knowing it has nothing to do with you.

This is Alpha.

Ask Yourself

» Recall the most recent experience where someone tried to make you feel stupid or worthless. Explain the emotions that arose. Anger? Confusion? Rage? Sorrow? Embarrassment?

» What do you think your tormentor felt at the time?

» How can you use compassion to break feedback loops in your personal or professional life? Try one approach today, with a partner, child, coworker, employer, or someone who tends to irritate you.

» What will you try? Compassionate listening? Thoughtful questions that put it back onto them? Do you feel they are too self-absorbed in their own madness to truly care about what they are making you feel? Or are they so cruel they intentionally want to harm you?

» Are you dealing with a narcissist? How can you feel compassion for them? Can you see they will miss so much wisdom and clarity of life in their lack of introspection? Does that allow you to have compassion for them?

COMPASSION AND #METOO

The New Alpha male understands he loses absolutely nothing by holding compassion for another. He loses nothing by helping and supporting a woman's empowerment in any situation—economic, social, political. Nothing.

Any man who cannot be happy for the success of a woman is a man who is emotionally stunted in a world of fear. Fear that was conditioned in him by figures who withheld love from him if he didn't win the game or get into that Ivy League school. Fear that was conditioned in him when he saw the beautiful girl choose the guy with the money or letterman's jacket. Fear that he wouldn't be "man" enough.

We can shame men for having this fear, which only makes them hunker down further in chauvinistic reaction. Or we can talk to them with compassion and share a space to be vulnerable, knowing that many men were raised by fathers and even mothers who withheld love and affection if they didn't "man up."

This does not mean we condone or allow misogynistic behavior. *No*. It means that while we hold men accountable and demand equal wages and respect for all in the workplace, we do so with clarity and compassion, not with social shaming tactics. Shame sends people's true selves into the shadows where grudges fester in wait for the right time to even the score. Publicly shaming a fear-based man will likely cause him to be publicly contrite but not inwardly reflective. Systemic change is a long game.

We can have compassion and still be firm—holding compassionate boundaries. For example, we can be compassionate toward people whose jobs are at risk, letting them know it is okay to be vulnerable and exposed, and also letting them know it is not always realistic or adaptive to demand that those jobs come back. Compassion is hitting people with the hard truth, helping them let go of stories and adapt more quickly, because telling people an untruth, even if it is what they want to hear, is not compassion. True compassion pushes people to the mirror of self-reflection and internal accountability, which is where they can begin to grow and adapt.

The world is changing, and we can't reverse nature and evolution, just like as a basketball player, I couldn't beg the officials to go back to calling the game the same way they were in the first quarter.

Being firm yet compassionate, we must show men that there is great courage in the willingness to adapt. It is essential, not only for the survival of society but for our species.

Many men are struggling to reconcile the #MeToo movement with the old stories we grew up with that are still prevalent: be a man, dominate, make money, win the girl, raise a family, be the provider and protector of your home—or else you will be alone.

Would it surprise you if I told you that men who abuse that power and sexually harass women often do so from fear, because they fear someone will take their power? It is a deep fear that if they do not dominate, they will be dominated. If they do not conquer, they will be conquered, says their logic, and they will be viewed as weak. They believe women will then gravitate to other men who have power—triggering the primal fear that they will be abandoned and women won't want to mate with them.

It all comes back to fear.

We never pardon horrendous acts of sexual aggression—*never*. However, we may begin to recognize how the frailty of humanity and the ills of the world are so often rooted in fear. Greed, violence, anger—they are manifestations of fear. Some men have behaved so atrociously in that fear-based mind-set that the idea of giving them compassion can be revolting, but we do it anyhow because we are brave enough to give it—not because it is fair. If you are giving compassion in hopes of receiving it back, it is not true compassion. When you get caught up in tit for tat, you lose sight of the long game, failing to see the intrinsic reward of compassion: boundaries and peace.

Overcorrection has never once in the history of the world brought about true systemic change. It only triggers further reaction, more overcorrection, and a pendulum shift back to the opposite extreme. Nelson Mandela, Mahatma Gandhi, and Martin Luther King Jr. are fine examples of people who did their best to stop the continual seesaw of overcorrection, choosing moderation, compassion, and love in their efforts to bring lasting, systemic change.

Whether it is patriarchy or feminism, disempowering others for your own empowerment is not empowerment, but rather reaction and scarcity mentality, which are merely symptoms of patriarchy. True empowerment holds no room for scarcity mentality. True empowerment is being allowed dignity while still holding the space for others to have theirs as well.

A newly empowered Alpha male understands that he loses nothing by showing compassion to the women in his workspace or family, to be an ally the women in his life can trust. This is especially important when it comes to standing up against sexual harassment in the workplace. The New Alpha male understands that supporting women in their ascension will not diminish his stature or shrink his power, for if any movement's "taking the power back" means oppressing another, it is not empowerment but, again, scarcity.

Through accountability and compassion, we can begin to allow men the space to be authentic and vulnerable. As we are being asked to adapt and empower women to become more represented in political and corporate leadership, may we also allow men the grace to have the space to work on and decode what is literally a survival imprint: *If I can't protect and provide, I will be all alone. Abandoned.*

Just as it is crucial for the feminine power to rise in station in our spiritual and evolutionary process, it is also essential for the New Alpha male to rise. And it takes all genders. It's a team effort.

It requires men to be bold enough to listen and hold compassion for women, just as it requires women to be bold and hold compassion for men. It requires extreme grace from the women in our culture who have been wronged for too long to demand accountability while stopping short of an eye for an eye. In that gap just short of full retribution is where grace abides. This act of compassionate grace creates systemic change, ending the cycle of retribution.

Compassion is the hardest principle. When you hold compassion and compassionate boundaries for a man who is stuck in an emotionally stunted world of fear manifested when he says misogynistic and hurtful things, you are able to keep his projections outside of your mind, knowing it is not about you.

It takes both masculine and feminine to evolve into higher consciousness, as equals of the yin and yang. For if there is no masculine to balance the feminine, we would see an imbalance to the opposite. It requires both men and women to empower us with accountability, while still allowing us to feel empowered as men and women.

If a man chooses not to do the work of evolving in this #MeToo era, we do not have to tolerate his intolerance. The New Alpha male does not tolerate bigotry, for fear cannot coexist in the world of compassion, which is where the New Alpha male resides.

For the men who are trying to adapt, they must be allowed grace and a margin of error as we face maybe the toughest ask of the male species in the history of our humanity. As the good men in this world fight for and honor women, we ask that women still honor us as men. For we need to be men.

It takes everyone to help the New Alpha male ascend, and it will not change overnight. This isn't simply a frontal lobe rewiring and conditioning. We are talking thousands of years of base survival—brain stem evolutionary conditioning. It takes time.

It takes compassion not only from men toward women but also compassion from women toward men. It requires the visible action point of men taking the time to sit with their female coworker for coffee, with no guile or ulterior sexual motives, to simply sit as a peer and hold the space to allow her to express her concerns and unease with the double standards that say men who show aggression are alpha and women who show aggression are bitches or too emotional. It requires men to let their female coworkers know they have their backs.

Conversely, it requires women to sit with their male friends and let men know their fears and anxiety are seen and valid. It requires women to help their male friends figure out new communication habits and physical reads.

Patience and compassion are required from all genders, to allow this old hypermasculine alpha societal coding to evolve and create space for equality where all genders speak a new truth, from the heart, knowing we all are equal, for we all are one. And one is all.

This is Alpha.

SELF-COMPASSION IN RELATIONSHIPS

There is a common misunderstanding that in the early days of Mormon history, Joseph Smith and fellow founders of the Mormon faith only practiced polygamy because there was a shortage of men to match the overpopulation of women converts.

It's a cute narrative—but untrue.

The truth is that there were fairly equal numbers of men for women, but many women chose to marry men who were the most devout and likely to ascend the church ranks because of their piety or leadership abilities—even if the man was already married. Many women chose power and comfort over the idea of love. Growing up in polygamy, I saw firsthand many women choosing status, power, and comfort over intimacy. There were enough pretty women married to one powerful man, especially the men who were "going places," to create the glaring discrepancy and reality. This occurrence instilled a true fear in me as a boy. A fear that said: the woman will choose the best man, the most powerful man. The alpha.

It was a visceral fear—one that gave me crippling anxiety whenever I saw a cute girl and prevented me from talking to her for fear that she might reject me. For if she rejected me, it would confirm I was not an alpha, such was the simple logic in my young, developing mind.

Thus, I didn't talk to girls growing up, partly because it was difficult for me to hear them with their higher-pitched voices, but also because of the fear that they would reject me. My first kiss was on my eighteenth birthday, when my parents and friends worked together to get me said first kiss.

This anxiety around girls followed me into adulthood. I avoided real intimacy and long-term relationships all throughout my twenties. When I got married, I lived in terror that my wife would be unhappy and the marriage would end, and that would mean, in my old programming, that I wasn't "man enough" to keep a woman happy. After all, my grandfather was able to keep seven women happy, and I can't keep one happy? What did that say about me as a man? And so I tried to be a robot, and stonewall, and play a role I thought she wanted. It didn't work.

That reality of a broken marriage came true, partly because of my own self-fulfilling prophecies and the mirrors we both played for each other. After that, I had two choices: run from the story that women would reject me if I wasn't powerful, which only would keep repeating itself in future relationships, or learn to face it head-on. At first I tried to ignore the story, but the fear was still palpable while I was transitioning into this new career as a motivational speaker, living in a basement apartment.

I was afraid to date, for not only was I still grieving and healing from my divorce, but I was also afraid, from these old stories, that a woman would see I lived in that basement apartment and would laugh at me and deem me a fraud who had nothing to offer her. Most men I know would rather die than face that kind of rejection.

During that time of humility-inducing living conditions, I began truly working on my spiritual wellness and gravitated toward a woman, with whom up to that point, I had shared the deepest spiritual connection in my life. We were on the same page about everything spiritual, as I began to explore the deeper layers of the metaphysical through the process of grief opening so many doors into my subconscious. She and I shared a beautiful connection, one that I will always be grateful for.

Then a richer man found her on Instagram.

And suddenly she was gone, living in Manhattan.

My old, deep fear had come true. It blindsided me because the entire time I never once believed that the material comforts mattered to her more than intimacy. It hurt because it brought up the deep-rooted fear and story within me—that women gravitate to the man who can best provide, not necessarily the man they can be most intimate with, despite all the Hollywood movies telling us otherwise.

I had a choice in that moment: I could angrily label all women as manipulators who say they want intimacy yet are truly gold-diggers who want material comfort, which had already been reinforced when I made the NBA and women who hadn't given me the time of day suddenly became interested in me. Or I could have gratitude for the woman who left. Her departure for finer things than what I could offer brought my deep fears and stories of masculine self-worth to the conscious level, forcing me to face them with accountability, integrity, and self-compassion.

You lose nothing by giving compassion to another.

Accountability that said I was a willing participant, as I had been, at least subconsciously, chasing and attracting women who would confirm this internal story and belief structure about women, power, and intimacy. Accountability that said I was the creator of my own self-fulfilling prophecies. Integrity asked that I continually integrate all aspects of my psyche into one cognizant and consistent person. Compassion for myself was essential as I learned to face my profound fear of abandonment and to give myself the love and validation that I thought had to come from another person.

A man doesn't need to grow up in polygamy to have this deep-seated fear of abandonment. We are ingrained early, when we see unattractive rich men walking around with youthful beauties on their arms. With this new wave of romantic entitlement, there is a delicate dance men are being asked to do—be vulnerable, but still be manly. But not too rough and manly.

I have fallen into this trap in relationships.

A woman told me she wanted me to be vulnerable and show my emotions. Yet when I showed too much, she was then afraid I was too tender and thus unable to be "man" enough to provide for her. She dumped me later that week. Overcorrecting, the next time a woman asked me to be vulnerable, I didn't show much, and thus she said I wasn't in touch with my emotions. She, too, called it a day.

I learned that most men and women want the same thing—someone who will communicate, not project. It will take time, and also authentic and compassionate communication from all genders, to allow men the space and permission to evolve.

While it isn't literally "Damned if we do, damned if we don't," it is a narrow passage we are being asked to walk as men. And we need help in doing so. We need women to support us. In a world of polarity, we have forgotten we are on the same team, men and women. It is a team effort. It takes compassion and communication, like all good teammates display.

It takes men owning their fears of not being "man enough" to learn to no longer react and overcompensate against such fears by degrading women, instead choosing to be brave enough to talk about it, regardless of whether an emotionally unavailable woman sees you as weak for being too vulnerable. Furthermore, it takes men showing compassion and acknowledging women's counterpart fear, which is that men will leave them for the prettier girl, along with their subsequent fear of powerlessness that accompanies such abandonment, which says they will be unable to survive on their own due to unfair wages.

It takes women offering compassion and owning the societal reality that many women still do chase material comfort and luxury over intimacy and equality. And that this truth is where many men are confused, even harboring deep subconscious resentment, unable to trust this evolutionary transition and let go of the old hypermasculinity that seeks fleeting power and shallow love.

It takes powerful moments of great empathy and compassion, like one I shared with my friend, a woman who has experienced extended professional abuse from men in her world as a public relations expert. This was shortly after my spiritual romantic flame had disappeared to New York to be with her new lover. On a park bench, my friend and I sat together, and I explained this experience.

As my friend heard me, she simply said, "That's shitty. I'm sorry."

This compassion is what heals the world: the discomfort of being able to hold compassion and intimacy toward another while still holding space for your own pain and trauma as you work through it. It takes those who have been greatly wronged to be the bravest of all—to demand accountability but stop short of full retribution and instead choose grace and compassion as my friend did for me. It takes the incredible discomfort of those who deserve justice to be the first to give compassion.

This is Alpha.

COMPASSION BEYOND BORDERS

Do you choose anger and entitlement, or do you choose compassion and empathy?

A New Alpha chooses compassion.

I have lost job opportunities when coaches discovered I had severe hearing loss and couldn't play with my hearing aids in. Rather than feeling I was owed something for my experience of being marginalized, I chose to extend compassion. This helped me empathize with my teammates who had a different ability, skin color, or country of origin from mine. And when they shared a story of racism or bigotry with me, I was able to say with empathy, "I am sorry. That sucks to have to experience that."

You lose nothing by giving compassion to another.

You lose nothing by hearing another person express rage and frustration about how terrified they are when pulled over by a police officer. You lose nothing as a man by showing compassion to another, by walking and envisioning a mile in their shoes. Yet, many men avoid the courage and bravery it takes to extend compassion—to understand why another man would feel the need to take a knee during the national anthem. Instead of giving compassion, many choose to twist the words of those less fortunate, those who live in real physical fear of death at the hands of law enforcement or immigration officials, and shame them. No compassion at all but stone-cold shame because these men fear they will lose ground or privilege by giving compassion to another. Yet compassion won't take privilege away; the realities of economics have already done so. The end of the life of privilege happened when we became an online world, enjoying immediate gratification and cheaper consumer deals and neglecting the long game. We can't spend all day shopping and communicating in a globalized world and then turn around and yell, "Build a wall!" You can't have it both ways.

Those days are gone. Sorry. Double standards are the antithesis of integrity, accountability, and compassion.

Playing basketball on all the continents, making many friends from such different backgrounds and walks of life, not to mention seeing pure abject poverty, I learned how lucky I was to grow up in rural Montana. Even when my family had no money after we broke away from polygamy, my life was pretty damn good in the worst of times compared to what I witnessed in impoverished communities in South America.

I am a lucky man, privileged even, due to all the travel that the American Dream presented to me, because life has pushed me out of my comfort zone, out of my bubble, and forced me to see the world in constant collision with other perspectives. These experiences did not make me ashamed to be an American, but rather proud: that a deaf polygamist kid like me could have even a modicum of a chance to go and chase his dreams. What a gift. Mark Twain said it best in *Innocents Abroad*: "Travel is fatal to prejudice, bigotry, and narrow-mindedness."

(Note: Five-star resort hopping is not traveling, my friends.)

In our globalized world many men are still trying to hold onto the illusion that the American Dream is exclusively theirs, and they fear they will lose it. Rather than clinging and trying to avoid the inevitable tectonic shifts of the global economy, they might want to consider sharing the American Dream with the rest of the globalized world, as ambassadors, empowering others with their own modicum of a chance to chase their dreams. Or, hell, even just eat, wear shoes in winter, or have a roof over their heads.

For me, being an American was not wearing a cowboy hat—or any hat, for that matter—and saying we are God's country or greater than any other. I gave up that cult mentality and tribal-nationalism when the illusion of being God's chosen people crumbled around my family. Once that happened, my habit of self-aggrandizement and the "othering" of people crumbled. Instead, being an American means traveling the world and sharing the story that was me, a kid with 80 percent hearing loss, who were it not for the incredible technology of hearing aids and the education system that was able to train me to speak would not have been able to do what I did with my basketball career. It means sharing the American Dream with others, knowing it wasn't mine to hold onto from a place of lack, like Gollum's "precious" ring in *Lord of the Rings*. It means continually reaching out to connect with others from different cultures, to break bread, barriers, and walls and connect the human spirit, no matter our backgrounds.

That is America. Abundance, not scarcity.

This is Alpha.

Do the Work

Practice compassion daily and notice the boundaries and the quick ability to detach from people's drama.

» The next time you find yourself in a situation where someone might be dumping or projecting onto you, go into observer mode. Get outside of your body and watch the moment.

» Allow them one minute—sixty seconds. See them with clarity, knowing your value and worth are not attached to how they are seeing you. You will resist the great temptation to interrupt or defend yourself. (If they are calmer and their energy isn't unbearable, you can wait for as long as your peace of mind allows.)

» When sixty seconds are up, and you can feel they are close to finishing, you may wait. When they are done, you will say, "Thank you for the feedback."

» And you will earnestly look for any truth in their projection, asking yourself if there is truly something in their projection that can help you see a blind spot you have.

» If their mental unwellness is to the point where they are not stopping, you will raise a prayer hand to them, and bow. This will interrupt them when your compassionate boundaries say their time is up. You will then say, again, "Thank you for the feedback. This is helpful."

» This will most likely enrage them. And if they continue to verbally assault you, you do not have to stay any longer. They will most likely see and understand that was your limit, your boundary, and respect it and/or grow bored with you, knowing you will not be a future choice to vent at because you will not give them the reaction they wanted.

» If they happen to threaten and/or become physically violent, then you can call the police. Whenever a player threatened me physically on the court, it never fazed me. I simply stared right back at them, saying, "What are you gonna do? Punch me? Cool, do it, and I will have fun watching you get arrested and suspended. And I will finish this game tonight and win it." They never threw the punch. And I never took the bait.

» Spend time daily imagining yourself in another's shoes, someone with a different skin color, religion, or gender, feeling what it must be like in their experience of the human condition without judgment or comparison to your own. Compassion is a muscle that requires development.

In the Zone

» As you settle down for this meditation, once you have relaxed into your heart drumming, lay on your back. Let your hands and feet rest comfortably.

» Take several quick and shallow breaths for one minute.

» Then, begin to pace each breath—a little slower and longer than the one before, until it takes you ten seconds to take a full breath. Once you are in that stage, focus on the color green.

» Think of how comforting green is wherever you see it in this world. Imagine yourself laying on a field of grass. As you feel yourself begin to relax, notice a small tree begin to root up from your chest, your heart space. With each breath watch the tree grow taller. Keep breathing until the tree is so high that you wish you could climb it.

» That tree is your heart reaching up to the sky and stars, breathing oxygen along with all the unconditional love it needs. It takes that free, endless love and oxidizes it to provide shade and shelter for all of those you love.

» See and notice all the people under the branches of your heart tree. Who is there? Are they all invited? Are there any who you don't want there? Why do you think they are there?

» In this moment, with all the people in your life who have had an impact standing under the shade that is your heart tree, take the time to look at all of them, and tell them "Thank you." Even the ones who hurt you—you look at them with compassion and give them even more shade and love, because they need it the most. And whether or not they say thank you, your shade does not lessen, because it is the sun that decides that, not humans. As the sun gives of its love and warmth so freely, unconditionally, you see with clarity that you cannot in good conscience turn around and withhold unconditional love from others. Not only do you give love to those who inflicted pain on you from their own madness of pain, you also look at all those who you have hurt and let down, giving both yourself and them compassion.

» As you show them with a smile how much you love them, allow them the space to see you with clarity and compassion, to see that you were doing the best you could in the moment of madness where you hurt them.

» Love them. Because you can.

RECAP

Compassion protects us. It gives us the clarity to see that people inflict pain because they are in pain. Compassion gives us the clarity of knowing where our boundaries truly are and what stories can be released. In that clarity, we understand that when people attack us or project onto us, it has nothing to do with us; rather, it's their own fear. This clarity allows you to play on. Compassion gives us greater depth of human connection, which leads to greater leadership. Compassion allows us to find intimacy.

This is Alpha.

HALFTIME

6

DISCOMFORT

The Fourth Principle of Perseverance

IT IS NOVEMBER IN BOISE, Idaho, and I am sitting on the training table in a cold, empty YMCA gym on day two of tryout week for the NBA minor leagues, where I am competing for the lowest-paid spot on the team. I arrive half an hour before everyone else. I sit on the table and take off my shoes and my socks, which peel off the bandages on my feet. I wince in pain as the torn callouses on the balls of my feet begin to bleed. Callouses that built up resistance over years of chafing and blistering of skin, through hundreds of pairs of shoes discarded when their rubber was spent. Callouses built by evolutionary design to make sure my skin didn't flay again. Callouses that helped me walk, run, and sprint so many miles toward my dream—now being discarded like the many shoes before, done in by my current shoes that I wore the year before in Europe. Shoes that should have been discarded a long time ago but weren't because I couldn't afford a new pair until yesterday after practice, when I got $30 per diem meal money and used five of those dollars to buy ramen noodles and the other twenty-five to go to a discount shoe store and buy a new pair of basketball sneakers.

The callouses were worth far more than the most expensive shoes in the world. It was a heavy cost, but I would have paid even more if that was what it took. I would have endured any amount of discomfort in pursuit of my dream.

DEFINING DISCOMFORT

Discomfort is necessary to the New Alpha male. It pushes us to the brink or even beyond, toward complete breakdowns, the kind of breakdowns that lead to breakthroughs. In those breakthroughs, we find clarity.

Comfort is the space where all your senses are relaxed. Discomfort is the act of being in and navigating spaces beyond comfort, where your senses are no longer relaxed by the physical, mental, emotional, or spiritual comfort zones. Nothing new or mind-blowing there.

What is mind-blowing is that so many people want their dreams to come true yet are unwilling to endure discomfort. Discomfort is the wager, the risk we ante up in pursuit of our dreams and goals in this life. Growth does not happen if we are not stepping outside our comfort zones, if we are not wagering a risk.

Discomfort is also the emotional and spiritual strain of learning to hold ourselves accountable for all our actions, thoughts, and stories. It is learning to move through the world with integrity, owning all aspects of ourselves as we remain the same person in every room we walk into, knowing some may not like all that we are. Discomfort is choosing to step out of our own bubble to hold compassion for others, knowing the world is not all about us. All of the Seven Principles of Perseverance require great discomfort. They force us out of our comfort zones. And the New Alpha knows that is where the magic happens.

Everyone says they want the American Dream.

But what price are they willing to pay for it?

How uncomfortable are you willing to be to get what you want out of life?

How willing are you to fail?

Everyone wants success and the American Dream, but few are willing to pay the price for it: hard work, uncertainty, risk, setbacks, disappointment, heartbreak, and many other experiences that fall under the definition of discomfort.

We see people wanting to avoid discomfort in the massive consumerism of "shortcut" books, purporting to be self-help by allowing people to think that a few quick tricks or positive thoughts will radically change their lives.

People want it easy, not just for themselves but for their children, in their effort to shield them from the necessity of discomfort and potential disappointment. Helicopter parents, in their efforts to protect their children from heartbreak, are not developing a threshold in their children for the discomfort of dealing with the real world when they come of age. They are actually doing them a disservice.

We have become not only impatient with but also intolerant of the necessity for process. I was willing to toil in the NBA minor leagues, making $1,100 a month, in debt, living off of ramen noodles, playing through great stress and discomfort to chase my dream. It wasn't always fun. It wasn't always pretty.

Perfection is not pretty.

We have detoured in our assumption that in order to achieve perfection we must immediately be perfect. And so most of us give up way too early on our dreams, thinking talent is more important than hard work. On the contrary, hard work is the greatest talent of all. If everyone could work hard, they would.

Where there is no struggle, discomfort, setbacks, or resistance, we cannot grow. Perfection is the daily choice of pushing yourself, awkwardly, out of your comfort zone.

Perfection is the art of aligning with discomfort.

It takes a special combination of grit and insanity or even naiveté to live in the unknown, beyond our comfort zones, in pursuit of the dreams we say we want. I admit I am fortunate in that my threshold for discomfort is high, in that early on my mother pushed me outside of my comfort zones every day by making me wear hearing aids and go to speech therapy. That daily battle gave me a high tolerance for discomfort, learning that is where magic and growth happen.

▊ Perfection is not pretty.

Are you willing to step beyond your comfort zone, not for a night but consistently, day in and day out for weeks, months, even years, not knowing where your next paycheck is going to come from? Are you willing to have people criticize and doubt you, even have some who want to see you fail?

How much discomfort are you willing to endure? How much instability are you willing to risk, to have your dreams come true?

UNDERDOGS

During the fourth quarter in a loud arena, everyone is deaf. And in the land of temporary deafness, the permanently deaf man is king.

But you have to play into the fourth quarter. Most people quit by halftime, as the discomfort is too much to bear. The underdogs who triumph, who inspire us, are the ones who are willing to do anything necessary to ascend and earn their place in history. Their desire to rise in their moment overcame the lure of staying in a comfort zone. As an underdog, if you hang around long enough, you stop being the underdog. But, you have to be willing to keep showing up. Half the battle is simply showing up, day in and day out, even if you have no idea when your moment will come.

This is what underdogs do. We stick around long enough and eventually the tables turn, at least for a moment. And then we seize the opportunity—but you have to play into the fourth quarter.

When I first got picked for the Idaho Stampede, it turned out I only made the team to be the media guy. You know, the guy who did the radio and TV interviews and also spoke to kids at schools. I was given the demeaning job, or so I thought at the time, of having to be the token guy at the end of the bench who had to go and do all of those things deemed beneath the other players.

It was a hit to my pride. I knew I could play ball and I was good at it, but my coach at the time didn't see it the same way. There I was, sitting at the end of the bench, hungry, not playing for weeks on end, making meager pay, reading to kids at schools, saving whatever money I could to pay off medical bills from my knee surgery following my first year overseas. You can understand why I was so excited when we went on the road, because that meant $30 per diem meal money. I could have easily ended my discomfort and said, "To heck with this! I am better than this! I am going to go back to law school," or something to that effect. Instead, I said this: "Fine, watch me. I am going to learn how to do a TV interview and radio interview. I am going to learn public speaking by talking to kids at these schools. I am going to learn these things so well that they will allow me to transition out of basketball and make more money than I ever did as a basketball player." And I did.

If you are working a job you feel is beneath you, and you are being pigeonholed, take that opportunity as the underdog to learn everything there is to know about that job. And then everyone else's job. When you are lurking beneath the radar, learn how to do those jobs so well that when you are promoted or start your own company, you know how to do those jobs better.

When people underestimate you, they are giving you the tactical advantage.

Later on in that Idaho Stampede season, the starting center broke his leg and the backup center got recalled to his NBA team, so by default I became the starter. In my first game as a starter on the road, I gave them thirty points and ten rebounds. I had known my opportunity would come if I stuck with it long enough, if I accepted a little discomfort. What kept me going through so much self-doubt was that I believed in the laws of physics—for every action there is an equal and opposite reaction. And so, if I kept putting in . . . and putting in . . . the universe would return the energy and give me a shot. Maybe one shot. That was all. And so I was going to be prepared for it.

How was I able to play for forty straight minutes after riding the bench for so many weeks? I made practice time my game time. Instead of pouting during practice, I made sure I touched the line on every sprint and always got that extra stride in while running with teammates during drills. Even when my teammates were ahead of me for the fast-break layup and didn't need my assistance to finish the play, I still ran with them, and even after they made the layup, I went one stride further and touched the baseline. Always the extra stride, so that if and when my number was called, I would be ready.

And my number was called. And I was ready.

For the rest of the season I averaged twenty-two points and thirteen rebounds a game.

To the basketball world, I came out of nowhere. Truth was, I was there the entire time; they simply chose not to see me. When they didn't see me, I had the choice to either feel sorry for myself or use my discomfort to blindside them.

That is the thing about being an underdog—stick around long enough, the tables will turn, and you will for a moment be the one with the advantage, like me in the fourth quarter in the loud arena.

As an underdog, or someone who feels they are undervalued or underestimated, you must always be willing to think outside of the box. You must learn to be comfortable with discomfort.

You must be able to ask yourself:

How much discomfort am I willing to endure as I prepare and wait for my moment?

How willing am I to take risks?

Am I willing to step out on my own, if the moment calls for it?

Everyone says they want the American Dream, but few are willing to pay the heavy price of uncertainty. How willing are you to fail?

Instead of pouting, can I choose to see I have the tactical advantage when people underestimate me?

With my hearing loss and the daily discomfort of being made to wear my hearing aids, to learn to read lips and to speak, along with bullying and learning to rise through that, I developed not only a high threshold for discomfort but, more importantly, a high willingness to risk and fail. My willingness to fail and learn and get back up every time is what has set me apart from many other players. I am not afraid of failure. Failure to me means I am simply stepping out of my comfort zone.

I have failed so many times it would blow your mind. But every time I fail, I choose to get back up, one more time. Every time. It is my choice; it has always been my choice. The essence of perseverance is choice, and it is my choice to see with clarity that my worth is not attached to an outcome. It is always our choice if we are willing take full ownership of that truth and empower ourselves with the accountability of choice.

If so, then you won't be an underdog for long.

The old, outdated alpha male believes he is entitled to success, because he is. He believes the American Dream is an automatic guarantee, and he will throw a temper tantrum and blame others—immigrants or women—if his reality doesn't match his entitled expectations.

The New Alpha male does not believe he is entitled to anything. He understands the world owes him nothing except, again, his own self-respect. He has woken up from the old American story that one is automatically going to be successful because he is male, while understanding that the pursuit of the American Dream or any dream is possible. Furthermore, he understands that anything worth having, worth fighting for, will require discomfort.

A New Alpha male, at some point in his life, was, is, or will be an underdog.

Ask Yourself

On a scale of 1–10, how high would you rate your threshold for discomfort?

» Physical discomfort?
» Financial discomfort?
» Social discomfort?
» Lack of support from friends and family discomfort?

MANIFESTATION

Contrary to what many "shortcut" spiritual evangelists say in their selling of the "Law of Attraction," you can't just wish for a pony and expect a pony to magically appear. Same for a parking space. This dimension doesn't work that way. It takes disappointment. It takes setbacks and heartbreaks. It takes discomfort in manifesting our dreams. It takes resistance to grow.

Manifestation is grit.

The Secret/Law of Attraction logic of setting intentions and never fighting or swimming upstream against resistance is flawed, if not completely devious. As a basketball player, if I had decided I wanted to have the best season of my life and didn't do any training or conditioning to match that intention, I would have been wiped off the map. Resistance makes us stronger. There is a time and a place for "path of least resistance," but it cannot be a mantra. Nature demands ebb and flow.

If you are in constant surrender mode, then you have not struggled, and thus you are not experiencing the true grace that comes in that alchemizing process of true surrender. Most people, especially those who "go with the flow" all the time, are usually just appropriating the word "surrender" to escape accountability, to avoid pain, heartache, and loss, which are all necessary experiences of life, as, again, a broken heart is arguably the most valuable thing in the world.

Runaway Law of Attraction propaganda keeps people stuck in the self-defeating logic of poverty shaming that positions God to be Santa Claus, blessing those who are the most spiritual. This has also enabled wealthy "influencers" to be exalted as paragons of virtue—*for if they weren't already so emotionally and intellectually brilliant, not to mention spiritual, how else could they have manifested all that abundance?*

If anyone is telling you they can help you manifest your dreams/lead you to enlightenment and it will be simple so long as you follow their plan or system, run! You are talking to a charlatan who wants your money. And more likely than not, they are trying to manifest you as their first client to put into motion their delusion that they have magical manifesting powers.

Real manifestation requires grit and discomfort, not the bypassing of it.

INTIMACY

One of the most uncomfortable topics for a male to talk about, no matter how Alpha he is, is intimacy in relationships, be they professional, family, platonic, or romantic. That is because most of us don't know what intimacy is. While we might think we do, intimacy has become misinterpreted by Hollywood and adopted by mainstream society to be nothing more than role-playing.

For many, role-playing is an unconscious expectation. Perhaps because a movie defined it when a man embarrassed himself in public to show the girl how much he loved her. Or your parents showed you that a woman is supposed to stay at home and be with the kids for a strong marriage. Many believe that as long as they play those roles, they will get the same outcome and intimacy as the movies or their parents. And in these roles, which we have been conditioned to play by our communities and culture, we have become enslaved to assumptions and unspoken contracts.

What is an unspoken contract? It's a subconscious expectation that once you establish a relationship with someone, they are supposed to play a specific role that resembles what you witnessed in your conditioning and upbringing, giving you an often false sense of control and an ability to predict the outcome. It is a societal, familial, or romantic expectation, even though there is never a spoken agreement and almost no conscious awareness at all. Unspoken contracts are often unconscious transactional exchanges that offer us belonging, which we have mistaken for intimacy.

The most popular unspoken contract is that of the soul mate, in which so many people believe and project onto someone the burden of being able to magically read their minds, and thus they shouldn't have to effectively communicate. "If you were my soul mate, you would just get me." Having spent sixteen years in speech therapy, the ability to communicate is one of the things I am most grateful for, and yet so many people are looking for a soul mate they don't have to have hard conversations with. Intimacy requires the discomfort of raw vulnerability and deep communication.

The default unspoken contract I projected was that I would always be the nice guy, and if I gave my partner everything she needed, she was supposed to always be happy. This was both illogical and completely irrational. While it may be perfectly functional at the global level—if you give someone what they want, they usually will smile and say thank you—it is devoid of true depth and intimacy at the personal level. If you are expecting someone in a close intimate relationship with you to always give you the same reaction every single time, you are not asking for intimacy, but rather for an employee. A job hires and pays you to play your role.

Yet we do the same thing at home, when we aren't being paid to play cultural roles we believe are expected of us. We don't work at our jobs for unconditional love. We work for money—to live, to eat, to support our family, in a clear transaction of our labor in exchange for pay. Yet we bring the same pattern of role-playing into our home life, believing that said role-playing will foster intimacy. All genders are equal perpetrators of such projection of expectations and can express disappointment—or worse, are mentally or physically abusive—when their expectations are not fulfilled.

While the cliché is that men fear intimacy, what we in fact fear is role-playing. We fear being an actor in someone's story and world of expectations—stories and expectations that society, reality television, and movies have told us is intimacy. This role-playing, which says true love has to look a certain way, is, in fact, the opposite of intimacy, and can be claustrophobic or smothering—hence the fear of powerlessness. Who wants to play a role, to be an actor all the time?

Intimacy requires the discomfort of raw vulnerability.

Communication is a path to intimacy, but talking doesn't always equate to communicating. The body will always tell you more. People's energy will always tell you more. Good communication is not saying out loud that you expect your partner to know you well enough by now to discern your intentions and read your mind—that's talking and projecting.

Projections and expectations are the bricks and mortar that build walls on a foundation of unspoken agreements, separating us from true intimacy. Our subconscious believes our tacit contracts will allow us to avoid heartbreak, when they actually cause them. I have found great wisdom from relationship experts like John Gottman (author of many books including *The Seven Principles for Making Marriage Work*) and the related research and data available from the Gottman Institute, but I believe many people have begun to overcorrect in their attempt to quantify and predict human connection and romance in hopes of avoiding heartbreak, which is often our greatest teacher.

As a society we have come to believe if we aren't experiencing heartbreak and disappointment, we are "winning" at relationships by avoiding discomfort. It is the opposite: a broken heart means we are growing, because each broken heart tears off one more mask as it brings you closer to true intimacy with yourself. With true heartbreak comes the death of illusions of what happiness is supposed to be, and with this comes the death of expectations. We can finally get real with ourselves. And when you can finally get real with yourself, you can get real with someone else. That is intimacy.

Intimacy is seeing and sharing your cultural conditioning with another, with full transparency, understanding that if your partner disappoints you or even leaves you, it has no bearing on your worth and self-work. Intimacy requires the discomfort of checking stories and expectations you project onto others. Intimacy is discovered in respected boundaries and standards, not in the expectations and roles we have been conditioned to play.

Through all my fumbling and all my failures, and in choosing to learn from those failures, the best way I have found to attain true intimacy with a partner is to behave with full accountability for my own self. Accountability means attacking my stories and patterns, and the projections they spur, and when they reappear, gratefully acknowledging they served me for a time but no longer serve me, and I release them. Then, if appropriate, I share that work and self-realization with my partner. This is intimacy. When you own your flaws, blind spots, and projections, and expose them with full vulnerability, you can bring the most to a relationship.

True intimacy is allowing the people who are destined to come into your life to shine bright, as we are all mirrors, and never shrouding them with our expectations. When you allow others to shine as their authentic selves, they will reflect not only your beauty but also the many wonderful things you still have yet to learn about yourself. Whether these lovers and friends stay or leave, you release them from your projections, allowing them the dignity to grow and shine on their path.

True intimacy is the uncomfortable act of not placing the comfort zones of your paradigm onto the other. It is in the discomfort that you find intimacy. For without your comfort zones, without your role-playing, you are truly exposed. Who are you without all the masks you have been told to wear, all the roles you have been told to play?

True intimacy is loving someone beyond the roles others have asked them to play. True intimacy is loving and accepting all aspects of you, owning your strengths and flaws with accountability as you integrate with integrity and love yourself compassionately. Step into the discomfort of being real, vulnerable, and authentic with others and yourself. This is intimacy.

It takes a brave heart to truly love oneself. When you do, you no longer project expectations on others to "complete" you. Instead, you let someone into the essence of you, unafraid of whether they reject you, for you no longer reject yourself. It takes boldness to let someone in this deep. And to love them that deep, knowing they are not yours to control. You may possess their love, but you do not possess *them*. And whether they stay or go does not diminish how bright your love for them in the moment truly was and still is. If you truly loved them, you love them forever.

If you loved them conditionally, depending on their behavior, you only loved the role they played, not they themselves, and thus you will simply move on to conditionally love the next role-player, feigning intimacy through stage acting. With a true unconditional love, even if they disappointed your expectations, you know that is what they were there to do: to expose those expectations and fears you were blindly holding onto, keeping you from true intimacy—from yourself and from others. And you know that despite times of discomfort, your unconditional love only makes you both shine brighter.

Put that on a stat sheet.

STANDARDS VERSUS EXPECTATIONS

The great destroyer of intimacy is expectation: "If you love me, you will do this for me."

As we consider projections and expectations, it is important to clarify the difference between a standard and an expectation:

» Expectations are manipulative projections of perceived lack.
» Standards are nonnegotiable reflections of self-respect.

Few men have been taught the difference, because our cultures seldom make the effort to do so.

Think about this. When you ask someone, "Who is your favorite Disney princess?" you will get the usual: Ariel, Snow White, Belle, and let's not forget the girl-power Pocahontas.

But when you ask the same person, "Who was your favorite Disney prince?"

Crickets.

"Aladdin."

"He wasn't a prince."

"Oh . . . Simba?"

"A lion."

This is because our culture portrays the fairytale prince as one-dimensional: be brave, be bold, be dashing, be on time to save the day, to provide and protect. And have lots of wealth to take someone to your castle for the happily-ever-after once you slay their dragons. No need for conversation—we can figure out your personality and feelings later, if the need should arise.

Do we think boys didn't get the cue when they watched these cultur-ally iconic movies, heard these stories, clearly showing the expectations for males? Be bold and courageous, protect and provide—your feelings are not even worth covering. Be there. Save the day and fix all the prob-lems. And if you want the beautiful princess, a trophy to reward your success, you gotta be a hero, dude.

Have we ever thought about how much anxiety a boy might feel while watching these movies?

I have close female friends who have even admitted to me they were angry at their boyfriends after watching a romantic movie, because *their* boyfriend never did those things.

In this day of social media and the illusions of those couples that are always happy, traveling, and making photo-worthy memories, we have begun to treat "activities partner" as the most important criteria of a relationship, along with other nearly impossible expectations. Instead of focusing on finding an activities partner, seek out someone who will help you grow and learn more about yourself. Instead of looking for a partner who helps you stay inside your comfort zone, look for one who pushes you beyond the boundaries, not just physically but, more importantly, emotionally. Remember that if you are brave enough to go there, discomfort in a relationship is a positive sign. It means you are peeling off masks and setting yourself up for true intimacy. Does your partner challenge you to look within and begin to hold yourself accountable in your relationship, and not just if your couple's selfie garnered a lot of likes?

It goes deeper than that. When you approach relationships hoping others/*they* will heal a wound within you, will ease your discomfort, this is a sign that you still approach relationships in a childlike way, allowing unspoken expectations to settle like landmines to sabotage relationships. An adult, an Alpha, approaches relationships knowing they alone are responsible and accountable for their own mess and development while maintaining immutable standards of respect. A standard is not controlling others with your emotions, whims, and mood swings—that is the manipulation mechanism of expectations—but rather a standard is a boundary that honors both sides of a relationship.

Expectation	Standard
You will never speak to me that way.	I won't be spoken to that way.
You should want to do those things with me.	I enjoy doing these things for myself.
I need a man/woman who will treat me right.	I will always try to meet my own needs.
You make me so happy.	I choose to be a happy person.
I will make you happy every day.	I'll do my best to help your happiness.

A New Alpha male does not choose to be an actor on someone's stage. He does not play into stories and the expectations that ensue. He does not engage in codependent relationships that have been disguised as true love by Hollywood. The New Alpha male knows that those movies and stories never show us what happens the day after. He is a good man, who is there to help his loved ones but does not bow to the guilt triggers that come from expectations, or the consequences of failing to meet those said expectations. He does not bend to expectations. He holds his standards through his compassionate boundaries, neither of which he apologizes for, because they are one in the same—compassionate boundaries are standards.

Remember, standards are nonnegotiable reflections of self-respect.

Expectations are manipulative projections of perceived lack.

The New Alpha male is clear in his standards and does not apologize for them, as uncomfortable as it may be, recognizing that many relationships will be outgrown as he embraces the growth that comes from such discomfort. When push comes to shove, he will always choose to be alone, free to pursue his path toward clarity, over loneliness in a relationship where he must forsake essential parts of himself to belong. If anyone tries to emotionally blackmail or manipulate him with expectations, the Alpha does not give in, even if it means the end of the relationship.

This is Alpha.

MASCULINE VERSUS FEMININE ENERGY

Ugh, the *feelings*—vulnerability. Most men would rather give their arm instead of talk about them. Being in touch with feelings is a place of extreme discomfort, an outgrowth of so much cultural conditioning and shaming.

With my hearing loss, I wake at the slightest vibrations. I feel very deeply, and it is overwhelming. Not just physical vibration, but others' emotions and feelings that stir my own feelings, which were *not* welcomed in my ultrapatriarchal upbringing. I endured the discomfort of many bumps and bruises along the way to my eventual acceptance of feelings as a natural part of being human. In my effort to fit into the world, I began to mistake the ability to speak and hear for what made me human, when in truth, what makes us human is our ability to feel.

People remember what they feel, not what they hear.

We have glorified intellectualism in this information age, which, as I've said, is overheavy on logic, to the point where we assume that someone who is wealthy or financially successful must be smarter or wiser than the rest of us. Yet, the true predictor of whether someone will be successful in life, not financially, but in happiness, is a higher score on emotional intelligence tests—a higher emotional quotient, or EQ.

While my basketball IQ served me greatly and allowed me to compensate for a somewhat lower level of sheer athleticism than many of my peers had, it was my emotional intelligence and intuition that carried me further—the ability to read my teammates and my opponents through their body language, but to also instinctively know when to be more assertive (masculine) and when to be more passive (feminine). This masculinity and femininity are not exclusive to genders. Consider what masculine and feminine energy and their associated behavior looks like.

> **Feminine energy:** empathizing, allowing/acceptance, nurturing, flexible, intuitive, passive, seductive, fluid, flow

> **Masculine energy:** structured, logical, driven, rigid, aggressive, assertive, steady, grounding, penetrating, goal-oriented, achievement

It is a balance of both masculine and feminine that the greatest basketball players display. Masculine is knowing when to strike, when to go for the jugular. Feminine is knowing when to let the game flow and come to you.

Michael Jordan, the all-time great, displayed both masculine and feminine at crucial times on the basketball court. He used feminine energy when he passed off the ball to Steve Kerr and John Paxson for them to hit the game-winning shots for their respective NBA finals victories. It was masculine when Jordan knew to take the iconic game-winning shot in the 1998 NBA finals, the great "push-off" shot. He displayed masculine energy in clearing out his defender with force, and then shooting it with no fear.

Neither masculine nor feminine is more important than the other. Both are needed at the appropriate times. If I am in constant aggression, masculine, "pressing it," as it is termed in the basketball world, I will find myself in trouble when I never pass the ball, and will become predictable, thus easy to guard—a liability. If I am being completely passive, feminine, afraid to take risks by always passing the ball, never shooting, I will miss opportunities—easy to guard. Living and playing in either extreme will get you benched. We must learn to balance and integrate masculine and feminine energy, be it on the basketball court, at work, or with family. And we need to do so with integrity: listening to our gut and feelings and what they are telling you—when to watch, listen, and observe and when to express your feelings and assert yourself in each room you walk into.

Here is an example of how a healthy Alpha male can express his feelings: "I feel frustrated because I feel emasculated every time you want to tell me about your feelings; it seems you are listing all the things I am doing incorrectly. I don't feel your feelings, but rather your judgment."

There is a fine line between expressing how you feel and dumping on someone your projections and judgments for failing to meet your expectations. The New Alpha male, in expressing his emotions, does not blame or dump his emotions on others, nor does he tear others down or emotionally abuse them.

Authentic vulnerability is empowered ownership of your feelings and clear communication of the masculine and feminine energy balanced in your heart space. All genders struggle with this. Just because women may stereotypically be better at expressing their emotions does not mean they have the monopoly on communication; for men, it takes great work through the serious discomfort of the fear of shaming to get to this space of balanced and centered heart-space communication.

While the New Alpha male is comfortable in his balance of feminine energy with his masculine, he still wants to feel and be treated like a man. This might mean he loves to provide, to protect, to climb and build and create and achieve. He may love to hold a woman in his arms, to allow her to cry on his chest, feeling that he can protect her—not necessarily save her, but be there for her. Men, it is okay to tell your significant other that you would like this, that you need to feel this.

Men evolved into the creatures we are. We are bodies that feel what our evolutionary coding has produced. And when men are not allowed to feel that intimacy, they will act out, mistaking power for the intimacy they are craving. This does not mean I condone men behaving badly—men who are only chasing power to fill the void of intimacy that is killing them from within. It is, however, me emphasizing that it takes all genders to heal all genders and rise into a new level of consciousness, walking the path of the heart where the New Alpha freely and courageously loves unconditionally, without strings attached, and allows others to love him unconditionally—even if that love is so great and blinding that it burns.

That is discomfort: the overwhelming feeling in your heart of love and gratitude for all that is—so much so that it hurts.

This is Alpha.

Do the Work

Try to find one small thing to put yourself out of your comfort zone on a daily basis. It can be physical exertion and training, or inward reflection and writing in a journal. If you're an introvert, do something social that connects you with people; if you're an extrovert, sit silently in reflection for an hour. Maybe it means holding your tongue during the dinner conversation and not letting everyone know just how smart you are or how in the know you are when they talk about the latest social media app, even though it may feel like death by a thousand cuts.

Make this a habit. Write down one thing that you notice about yourself that if you had to do it would feel so awkward it would nearly constitute torture. And as you make note of that, find an opportunity to meet and outgrow it. Do this each day, and as you do, notice how the anxiety lessens and how your confidence grows.

The ability to be uncomfortable is a skill. Learn to step beyond your comfort, and you will see the growth and reward on the other side from a place of acceptance.

In the Zone

» After you have completed your round of heart drumming, lay face down on the floor with a towel as your mat.

» Stretch your arms and legs to four corners.

» With the first minute of breathing, focus on pressing your forehead into the towel.

» During the second minute, notice the pressure on your nose and neck.

» In the third minute, notice the pressure on your chest as your ribs work to expand.

» Notice the pressure on your pelvic bone as well as your knees in the fourth minute.

» By now your body should be uncomfortable. With each thought that comes into your head about how you want to switch over, instead say, "Thank you for letting me grow comfortable with discomfort."

» In another minute, you will finally roll over onto your back, keeping your eyes closed, noticing the sensation of your body moving the blood around. In that moment of clean circulation, hold the intention in your mind of how you will do something today that will make you slightly uncomfortable socially.

» Notice how it doesn't seem as scary as it normally would have, for you are developing the threshold of discomfort. It is a habit that turns into skill.

RECAP

Discomfort is essential in our growth and self-development. Without it, and without the sacred detours of life, our perspective will only be tunnel vision. Discomfort gives us the ability to have true compassion and thus intimacy with others as it leads us not only to greater heights and experiences but also to deeper places of loss and heartbreak, which set us up for the powerful skills of acceptance and surrender, which in turn leads to transformation.

⑦

ACCEPTANCE

The Fifth Principle of Perseverance

ONE OF THE MOST POWERFUL moments of my professional sports career was when I erupted and scored twenty-nine points in a second half after I'd been scoreless in the first. I remember walking into the locker room at halftime, going through my own self-abusive routine of replaying all my mistakes in the first half. "I missed my first seven shots. I am playing like garbage. I can't miss the next shot."

In that moment, a small voice came into my head saying, *You are only as good as your next shot.* I tried to reason against it, but continued, *You missed those first seven shots because that's what was supposed to happen.*

That's stupid, I said to myself. *Why was that supposed to happen? Because that's what happened.*

I accepted this and went back out and gave them twenty-nine points, knowing I was only as good as my next shot, knowing I was only a good teammate if I was present for my teammates. That moment of pure acceptance got me back into the present moment, where I was best able to perform.

DEFINING ACCEPTANCE

Acceptance is the powerful yet feminine act we take toward complete transformation into the New Alpha male. Because it is passive, we have mistaken it for weakness or quitting—it is anything but. Acceptance is the act that often appears as the only rational option after we have resisted changing our behavior long enough yet keep living the same painful patterns and experiences. Learn to recognize acceptance in its many manifestations:

> » Acceptance becomes your new reality when the discomfort of the old reality is no longer acceptable.
> » Acceptance is not just shrugging your shoulders and walking away from a challenge or responsibility. It is the graceful act of allowing yourself to see your challenge through a new lens.
> » Acceptance is the acknowledgement of what you can and cannot control.
> » Acceptance releases the pressure of resistance that has us caught in a feedback loop of frustrating patterns. It gives us clarity and empowerment in the present moment to make the best decisions moving forward.
> » Whereas quitting is a state of reaction, of giving up out of frustration, acceptance is clarity in the moment, knowing the limits and breadth of your control and empowering yourself with the accountability of choice within those boundaries. When we accept a current circumstance and allow it to be what it is, we develop clarity to make the most informed decision in the present moment with no stories clouding our judgment.

True acceptance is accountability in the present moment and not repeating the same pattern or mistake. Not being present, which is living in the past or the future, is not being accountable. Wallowing in past guilt, wishing you could change an outcome, is false accountability. It is nothing but a distraction from facing the consequences in the present, where accountability resides.

When we accept our reality, it is not because we are complacent or quitting. Rather, it's the opposite. Acceptance is key to perseverance.

HINDSIGHT IS NOT 20/20— IT'S A CHAIN REACTION

There is a cliché in the sports world that says you are only as good as your last game. I push back against this. I used to do this thing where I would go home at night and replay an entire game in my head. I would gnash my teeth with irritation: *Oh, if I had made that easy little hook shot in the second quarter, I would have had twenty points tonight and not eighteen. . . .*

One day, as I was turning thirty, I had an epiphany: If I had made that easy hook shot in the second quarter, the opposing team would have had to stop and inbound the ball and the next play would have been completely different and then the next play would have been completely different, and it would have gone on along a completely different chain reaction, so who is to say I would have even ended up with eighteen points? I might not have touched the ball for the rest of the game and only had eight points.

So, when people say "Hindsight is 20/20," this is incorrect.

Hindsight is a chain reaction.

When you think about it for a moment, every day we are living in a chain reaction of sequences far greater and beyond our power than any of us want to admit. We do not have as much control as we like to think we do. To think our reality would look a certain way "if only" something in the past had gone differently is even more naïve than wishing we could change the past.

As I've matured, I've had to accept that I have little control over my life, especially over things that have already happened. As I accept this truth and I flow in those present moments in which I am aware I have some control, I can find the clarity to make the best decision in that moment, which gives me the most control I can possibly have in my life.

Acceptance is empowerment.

That is how I matured as a basketball player in my later years. I no longer worried about the last shot I missed. The moment I accepted that I had little control and was clear where I did have a choice was when I had the most control over my life.

Repeat: When you accept that you have little control, you gain control.

This allowed me to play basketball for six more years around the world, and every year in my thirties I played, I was an all-star wherever I went because I knew what I could control. (Except, of course, for the occasional referee who was blatantly biased. Hey, I am still human!) The fact I could let things go and tell myself I was only as good as my next shot, not my last shot, allowed me to be consistent.

You are only as good as your *next* game. The past is gone. Let it go. Accept it. Learn and move on. Empower yourself with the clarity of the present. When you do you this, you will find yourself keeping your beat, not too high, not too low, able to acknowledge the outcome of a situation and detach your self-worth and learn from it and grow.

My self-worth is in the consistent beat I keep. Not in the event horizons or deep valleys. I have done "awesome" things and I have done "bad" things. I have triumphed and I have failed in endeavors. But that is not who I am—I am the person who keeps the beat through all the highs and lows, accepting those fleeting outcomes to be what they are and release them.

Sometimes the timing or bounces don't go our way. Sometimes the shots won't fall. Talk about discomfort. Contrary to New Age philosophy, it doesn't necessarily mean we have unresolved baggage. And contrary to the western masculine mind-set, it doesn't necessarily mean someone was more deserving than us. With acceptance, we learn to be happy when others find their success, knowing ours will come, too.

That is empowerment.

That is Alpha.

Ask Yourself

> » Think about a situation or experience that you struggle to let go of. Why is it so important to you?
>
> » What do you think it will mean or say about you if the situation were to magically go your way?
>
> » Think about dreams you had that were never realized. What did you tell yourself about yourself when those dreams didn't come true? Or when they didn't look exactly like you expected them to?
>
> » Do you understand the difference between acceptance and quitting?
>
> » Can you write two scenarios in your past when you accepted versus when you quit?

Acceptance means learning to be conscious and self-aware, not self-absorbed, asking and acknowledging where you have power and where you don't. This will allow you to navigate life far more smoothly despite the problems and challenges thrown your way, allowing you to save your energy for the battles that are winnable, and more importantly, worth fighting.

» Write down all the things you are trying to control in your life right now.

» Separate the items on your list into categories of what you can control and what you cannot. Simply seeing them in front of you, not in your head, will give you the permission to allow and accept your energy to be best applied to things that you can influence.

GRIEVING

The New Alpha male understands and accepts that energy is everything. Not just the mental energy of our emotions and what we put our physical efforts into to make our lives enriched and fulfilled, but, furthermore, that absolutely *everything* is energy. This is not simply an expression.

The space between a neutron and electron within an atom is so vast it may as well be empty space, and the only thing holding it together is energy. The illusion of those atoms rubbing together when we rub our hands is exactly that, an illusion, and what we are feeling is the friction of energy. As everything is energy, we must understand the sacredness of it.

Letting any organism that means to harm, control, or manipulate us invade our sacred space, mentally or physically, is a self-sabotaging act. The human brain and heart, as science has shown, emit electromagnetic waves. As they do so, they also receive energy as we move about this vibrational grid that is our dimensional reality.

» When we take the time to breathe and focus on our breath, we are grounding ourselves, charging up our senses, like plugging a phone into an outlet. We align with the energy in our body.

» When we exercise and put our body through resistance, we are building our energy reserve like water friction within a dam generating electric power.

» When we stretch, sweat, or cry, we are purging ourselves of stale frequencies and energy that needs to move.

» When we eat well, we are keeping the wirings and mechanics of our body clean and functioning at optimum ability. Just as food intake is crucial to the maintenance of your body, the energy you choose to carry in your heart is as crucial. You can be a healthy vegan, but bitter, angry, or condescending, and your health will suffer. When you choose to operate in the higher emotions, with gratitude being the highest energy level we can vibrate at, you are keeping your frequency pure— not to mention balanced in masculine and feminine—which is preemptive healthcare and maintenance, not damage-control maintenance.

Energy has to move. And while some people might be more skillful than others at moving energy, it is important to have a Swiss Army knife of possibilities. The universe, life, and even the game of basketball do not suffer one-dimensional folks well. If you are easy to guard and predict, you will be discarded. If you have a go-to outlet like meditation, yoga, or gym workouts and you suddenly can't do it that day and then your entire day is ruined—you have fallen into the one-dimensional game and you have become easy to guard—as you have no other coping mechanism to self-soothe. You have become dependent if not addicted to your one coping skill. Develop an array of skills and coping mechanisms and you and your body will not only adapt more easily to curveballs thrown at you, on the court and in life, but your brain will be happier as well. If you're hard to guard, you've developed coping skills that cover all dimensions of you—mind, body, and spirit.

For the first year after I retired from basketball, I was not kind to my body: I didn't exercise as much. For years, basketball itself was the main stressor in my life—the political and financial pressures that came with it. I made the error of connecting basketball and exercise itself as stressors. When exercise was my life for twenty years, I burned out on it. Yet over time, while I was going through my transitions, my health and happiness were on a serious decline. The stress of divorce and being a single father was taking a huge toll, my back and neck were aching, and a slouch was appearing in my posture—my entire structure was crumbling.

It doesn't take much to take care of your body, especially if you focus on its core. Furthermore, working on your core, through plank holds, balance drills, and medicine balls, rather than focusing on the vanity muscles, you are centering your body, which brings mind, body, and spirit into balance. Disease and dis-ease have come into my life when I have fallen out of that balance, especially when I did my best to avoid grieving.

Men are not often given permission to grieve. We are shamed at the earliest age for tears. In my community growing up, such outward grieving was viewed as a sign of lack of faith. I had to learn to how to grieve as a thirty-five-year-old man. I needed to give myself permission to cry, not with anger, but with acceptance that crying is a process of purging energy.

Breathing is possibly the most powerful tool for aligning with our acceptance of what is. It is the great conduit of grief. I began recalling some breathing techniques I had used before games, but this time in my quiet basement apartment, which became a cocoon for my metamorphosis.

When you accept that you have little control, you gain control.

Meditation doesn't make your problems go away. It simply puts them in perspective, with the clarity on whether you act or allow them to resolve themselves naturally. Not all meditation is silent and still. Any act of getting out of your head and into your heart-space, to walk the path of the heart, is meditation. Heart drumming is meditation. Painting or carving or any artistic pursuit is meditation. Playing basketball fully present is a form of meditation. Again, meditation is any practice that gets you into your body and centered in the present.

My path of struggling with Buddhist meditation led me to shamanic, or Native American, meditation, where drumming beats helps your mind go into a deep state of Theta consciousness. My brain responds much better to the drumming, with the permission to allow my consciousness to go where it needs to. Upon asking a sacred medicine woman, who was my neighbor in Montana, about meditation, she suggested that there is often great importance in what geographic region you were born in this life, in regard to the type of meditation that is best for you and what you will most respond to. Having been born in Montana, in the Bitterroot Valley, the legacy of Chief Joseph is strong. I remember as a little boy the first time I saw his picture at the museum; I was entranced. I loved him. His energy was there. I read all the materials, stories, and plaques. I went home with a book, in which I got to read all about Chief Joseph. To this day, Chief Joseph is my greatest hero. Although I am of Anglo descent, my connection to the land of Montana, where I was born, has always been stronger. I still feel the energy of the soil and the Bitterroot River. Even in all my travels across the globe, I can still feel Montana—it is my stargate.

Connecting to my early geography and becoming disciplined with a modality of meditation allowed my grieving and acceptance of reality to come full circle. I took up a guided meditation that begins by facing in the four cardinal directions:

North for Clarity and Ancestors
East for New Beginnings
South for Manifestation
West for Endings

As I face each direction in meditation, I call upon one of the elements:

Fire, walk with me as we purge what no longer serves me.
Water, carry me through the depths that few dare to tread.
Earth, ground me as I walk in beauty through all these
illusions around me.
Air, carry my words and intentions to all directions.

Each of the elements holds a great sacred power to help transmute energy—especially fire. In the sacred fire ceremony, you write a letter to someone you need to forgive, even if you feel they don't deserve it. You let the letter sit for a day, and the following evening, you burn it. During the grieving process for my divorce, I can't tell you how many letters I wrote and then released as I watched the fire carry my words to the stars. This is one of the most cathartic things I know, and I recommend you call upon the elements to help you move into acceptance—the completion of the grieving cycle.

The New Alpha male is brave enough to learn the sacred art of grieving, because grieving is the journey into full acceptance of what is. When we are in a place of acceptance, we can move and grow; when we do not accept reality for what it is, we get stuck.

In the acceptance of what is comes the clarity to see the collective ego and fear that drives most avatars and their stories in this world. Yet the New Alpha male does not judge, knowing that any false superiority is the same sin as what they would be judging: ego and fear. Instead, he only wants to help others release themselves from the illusions of this upside-down world. He learns to do so through allowing his heart to be a limitless source of unconditional love in the pure acceptance of what is—personal and impersonal at the same time, as it discriminates against none, knowing we are all children of the Great Spirit, as he walks the path of the heart.

Walking the path of the heart is living in constant meditation, in full acceptance of the world as it appears, always present as you respond gracefully to each maneuver around you with ease and acceptance rather than resistance.

This is Alpha.

ACCEPTANCE PRECEDES SURRENDER

Acceptance precedes surrender. True surrender. And I waited until halfway through this book to introduce the word *surrender*, as it is a word most men fear, believing it means "defeat." This false assumption about surrender could not be any further from the truth; there is great power in surrender, if we actually know what it is.

It's important to understand the distinction between acceptance and surrender:

> » Acceptance is a place of being in allowance of what is, so that we may best understand and utilize the current situation to gain the best possible or preferred outcome.
> » Surrender is complete allowance of what is and, furthermore, complete alignment with the truth of "whatever will be will be."

When I was in a place of acceptance on the basketball court and in my life, I still allowed myself hope and expectations of what the future was going to be. Like most of us, I thought I could twist God's arm and say, "Okay, God, I am surrendering, you can see me being a good boy now. And now you can give me what I want, because I am behaving well."

This false surrender is a child archetype that many of us still possess toward God or the universe or a Santa Claus figure: good behavior to receive an incentive like well-being, virtue, or presents. True surrender has no incentive other than peace and clarity. Ironically, true surrender gives you the greatest power.

I did not know true surrender until I found myself living in that basement apartment as a thirty-seven-year-old man. It was a winter night, and my son was up with a cold. I was worried about paying rent because money had stopped flowing even though things had gotten better in my life: my TEDx talk was doing well, and I was being booked for speaking engagements. However, my reality was severely clashing with my expectations, with the added insult of my single-dad-minivan being totaled from a spinout on black ice.

That winter night, while Simon was coughing his lungs out, I sat at my table watching my bank account bleeding dry from all the various business expansions I was trying to pull off. The only control I had (and I crave control myself) was to go to my little woo-woo corner, the fireplace where I kept my sage and oracle card deck.

I drew a card and it said, "Speak clearly and state your truth."

To which I replied, "You want my truth, okay . . . Fuck you!" And what followed in my temper tantrum only escalated from there, to whatever gods would hear me. If you are gasping shock at the sacrilege, don't worry. It's okay to have a temper tantrum when talking to your higher power. It already knows who you are. One hundred percent reverence is false reverence, which brings us back to the principle of integrity.

After I had cussed and raged for more than ten minutes with angry tears streaming down my face, I was exhausted. I lay down and began sobbing. Once I had voiced my true expectations, exposed them, no longer playing coy, I could finally release them. I was so tired. I wasn't sleeping at all due to the stress of my expectations.

True surrender has no incentive other than peace and clarity.

In that moment, once I had nothing left, no more resistance to give, no more expectations of what it was supposed to look like according to my terms, I finally found a place of surrender as I said out loud: "Not my will, but yours."

Without being a victim or a martyr, I remember saying, "If you want me to go teach high school history and be a basketball coach, I will. If that is where you want me, I will go." And I meant it.

In my grand according-to-Lance/Machiavellian scheme, I was going be a popular life coach and climb the corporate speaking ladder. And in said grand scheme, once I became "successful" enough, I would slowly show my true colors. I would unveil my spiritual side, my woo-woo side, but only after I had the voice of credibility to do so. It was a ten-year plan in my head.

Life had other ideas. Rather, it said, "You will pivot now. You will be authentic, and you will show your true colors, now. The world doesn't have time for such charades."

As I lay on the floor, I recalled a painting I had seen as a boy in a museum in Montana. It was of the Heyoka Warrior, the Sacred Clown of the Lakota, who rode into battle seated backward on his horse. American soldiers thought he was being a ridiculous clown, but they failed to see that the joke was on them, for while they were playing checkers for land in this dimension, the Heyoka Warrior was playing inter-dimensional chess. He was a living symbol of absolute trust in a higher power, a Great Spirit. Not a naivete that things will go their way if they wish hard enough but absolute trust and surrender that everything that will be, will be.

I saw the Heyoka, in my mind in that moment in my basement apartment, asking me to surrender in the bravest possible way: to get out of my own way with no expectations of reward or blessings.

To allow things to work through me.

To truly surrender to Creation, to be used however it wishes.

To surrender to the truth that, yes, I am a thirty-seven-year-old single father living in a basement apartment.

To surrender to the truth that, according to the cultural image of "success," I was a walking hypocrisy of a motivational speaker.

To surrender to the truth that, if I truly wanted to help others, I had to get myself out of the way.

To surrender to the truth that, if I truly wanted to inspire and help others, I had to take off all the masks.

To stop trying to logic and reason through life and allow mysticism room to enter and lead the way, which was more difficult than running a thousand suicide sprints.

To acknowledge that without a higher power, basketball trophy or not, I was nothing.

When you meditate and pray, do you truly accept and surrender to the message you receive, or are you only foolishly thinking you can twist God's arm to get your way on Sunday, like I did for far too long?

This is not to say we do not move about the world with intention and manifestation. We do. We are engineers. We work and we strive for our goals and our dreams, but then we bravely and completely, and I mean completely, detach from the outcome. We surrender all expectations of what the end result is supposed to look like.

Why would we work so hard in creating the life we desire without the promise of reward?

Because the greatest reward is the journey of self-discovery into those vast inner dimensions we travel while simultaneously walking this outer world, the upside-down world, in search of those fleeting material treasures that always lose their value, like trophies gathering dust on shelves, as opposed to the self-worth we find, or better yet, recover in places we least expect.

Always chase the dream. And somewhere along the way, you will learn that you are worth more than the dream itself.

Work and strive. Labor after your dreams. Always. Work until the work is done. When you can't work anymore, work a little more. And then painfully let it go, surrendering the outcome to be what it will be.

In truth, true surrender must be earned.

Many people, especially of the New Age modality, flippantly commandeer the word *surrender* without earning it, as a way to stay inside their comfort zones. While men are culturally coded to fix all the problems, the New Alpha male is challenged to persevere with the heart to help others, and then, after he has done all that he can truly do, surrender completely, unconditionally, with accountability and humility rather than expectations, so he can then watch magic reveal itself in new ways.

You may wonder why I don't call the fifth of the Seven Principles of Perseverance "Surrender," as basically that is what I am setting up acceptance to be.

Here is the answer: Because most men recoil in terror when they hear the word *surrender*. They believe surrender is synonymous with defeat. And so, as in this book and in coaching and keynotes, I have to gently guide them into surrender, allowing them to feel safe initially within the concept of acceptance. Then we can go deeper into surrender, aligning with the deep mystical force of all that is and what will be, to work through us.

Acceptance still allows the narrative to be about you.

Surrender allows the narrative to work through you.

True surrender is bowing to the greater good of Creation. This grounding peace of bowing to something greater than yourself, surrendering to Creation with clarity that everything is not happening to or even necessarily for you, but rather through you—that Creation is happening through you—is the most powerful space we can hold. This is the true standard and sign of winning, in the eyes of the Alpha male.

Surrender is aligning with oneness within you. This peace of oneness is established in the daily discipline and skill of always being in acceptance of what we can and cannot control. People will be drawn to that peace, some thinking they can buy it or take shortcuts to get it, but there are no shortcuts. Again, true surrender is earned, experiencing the painful loss of letting go after you have worked so hard. It takes great courage, possibly the most courageous thing a person can do, to surrender. Acceptance is a demanding daily discipline, a principle of perseverance, and only those with the gritty skill of self-reflection know how to dance with it, as they merge with the deep power of surrender, allowing all that will be to channel through them—wielding true power.

This is Alpha.

THE KNOWING FIELD

What does wielding the power of oneness to work through you look like?

It looks like the moment when you see athletes find themselves in the magical place of what we call "the zone," where things just are, and you are flowing with all that is, never forcing it or pressing it.

How can you get there?

Well before I understood what meditation was, I adopted a routine before games where I would look for a dark corner where I could lay on my back, usually while the other team's starting lineup was being announced. I didn't care if other people noticed. Sometimes I did it at the end of the bench, in front of the entire arena.

Once I found a spot, I began doing a breathing technique where I would slowly breathe in for ten seconds, hold it for ten seconds, and then breathe out for another ten seconds, taking thirty seconds each rep. I would envision an energy bubble around me as I touched my fingertips together and whispered, "This is my energy." I called it my "10-10-10" breathing.

Dear Sounds True friend,

Since 1985, Sounds True has been sharing spiritual wisdom and resources to help people live more genuine, loving, and fulfilling lives. We hope that our programs inspire and uplift you, enabling you to bring forth your unique voice and talents for the benefit of us all.

We would like to invite you to become part of our growing online community by giving you three downloadable programs—an introduction to the treasure of authors and artists available at Sounds True! To receive these gifts, just flip this card over for details, then visit us at **SoundsTrue.com/Free** and enter your email for instant access.

With love on the journey,

TAMI SIMON Founder and Publisher, Sounds True

ST330

Free Audio Programs!

The Self-Acceptance Project ($97 value)
Instant access to 23 respected spiritual teachers and more than 26 hours of transformational teachings on self-compassion, especially during challenging times.

The Practice of Mindfulness ($15 value)
Download guided practices by Jon Kabat-Zinn, Shinzen Young, Kelly McGonigal, Tara Brach, Sharon Salzberg, and Jack Kornfield.

Meditation Music ($10 value)
Listen to nine inspiring tracks for healing, relaxation, and releasing stress.

To download these **3 free gifts** go to **SoundsTrue.com/Free**

SOUNDS TRUE
many voices, one journey

800.333.9185

I did ten sets.

While I simply was trying to ground myself, I was unaware of all the other mechanisms I was triggering—most importantly, just getting me into my body and out of my head:

> When we are in our minds, worrying about the future or the past, we are not present, we are not in acceptance.

> When we are in our bodies, we are fully present and in acceptance of all that is in this moment.

If time was limited, I would take thirty "power" breaths, where I would intentionally focus on my breathing as I inhaled and exhaled as quickly and forcefully as I could, for thirty breaths. This got me out of my head and into my body quickly.

There were times in my career where I was angry and depressed and every game was a psychological battle, such was the state of the fear and culture of the team. And while it might have felt nice to *react* in the immediate short term and tell an official "what was what" and get that technical foul, it sucked in the long term when we lost the game. Unable to see the forest for the trees, I sabotaged myself many times, unaware of how much energy I was bleeding and giving to other people when I was in a state of reaction instead of peaceful action and response.

To cope and mature as a player, and most importantly, adapt, I began to do the breathing techniques before the game. When I did so, my body more than likely was going to play the game in the zone, a meditative state, from the heart, as we have been learning and practicing thus far with the "In the Zone" segments.

I couldn't play totally from the heart, and not without any logic, or else I would not have executed the set structured plays when the hand signals were called from the sidelines. Nor could I play totally from the head, because I would have detached from my body and begun to play from a place of fear and analysis rather than confidence and flow.

It takes both masculine and feminine.

While the head—logic, reason, and intellect—has its purpose and is essential, playing from the heart is far more important. When you hear players talk about playing in the zone, it is a magical place where you are so present in your body that you do not even think—you just are. Your brain has taken a back seat to your heart, intuition, and instinct. You do not aim your shot—you just shoot, trusting your body and physics to go where it will go. You observe everything with soft focus where you do not analyze, you do not critique, you just respond. You are "being," as you play from the heart, where things just "are," in full surrender of all that appears as a challenge, able to gracefully maneuver around it, in full trust of your own internal intuition channeling through you to counter in peaceful response. This is when you have stepped into what I call the "knowing field."

The knowing field is the true aim of meditation—being fully present, able to see your true soul self with clarity. Further, it is the presence to see your soul self as one with an entire grid of energy that makes up our matrix and the universe beyond. When we are balanced and present, we see with clarity that the defense of the opposition always has to give you something. Just like life always has to give you something. And with peaceful action, you take what is offered, and you move into a space of surrender—peaceful response, never with reaction.

The knowing field is the place Buddhist monks speak of when they refer to higher consciousness, stepping beyond the simulation, detaching our brains from the digital grid of ones and zeroes. It is a state of pure awareness: no past or future, just pure present awareness of all that is, where we know that each shot will fall in its perfect place, make or miss. A state where we see such knowing and flow that we do not miss a step, as we gracefully dance in rhythm to the tune of life, accepting what is and responding in perfect timing, pushing in one moment and surrendering in the next with seamless ease between masculine and feminine. This is true flow, which goes beyond merely not resisting. True flow is attacking and defending, taking and giving, struggling and relaxing in perfect synchronicity with the rhythm of life, ebb and flow, because you are life.

The knowing field was what I experienced when I stepped onto the stage to give my first TEDx talk. With logic and reason—the masculine mind—I had prepared all the words I needed to say. But once it came time to speak on that day in front of those thousands of people, my heart took over. I didn't even have to think. I had no fear about remembering the words, for if I had been remembering the words, it would have meant I was speaking from my head. Instead, I got in my body and let my body flow and tell the words to match its dance on the stage. Being in the knowing field meant logic and reason were no longer driving, but rather the heart carried the words. Whenever people paraphrase parts of my talk they enjoyed, they don't necessarily remember the words, but they remember what I helped them feel, via speaking through my heart, not the mind.

The zone is the beautiful space of seamless balance of taking what is offered and surrendering what is asked, knowing that for everything life takes from you, it has to give something back. The defense always has to give you something, and in that clarity, you find the zone, the place of no-*thing*, where nothing is permanent and everything is fluid. Where nothing is lasting, and everything is eternal.

Finding and playing in the zone is stepping into the knowing field, where things just are. Where you cannot truly put things into words, where you cannot try to logic and label, where you cannot aim your shots, for to try and do so, you would lose the knowing in your bones and the connection with the knowing field. Only in surrender—in full acceptance of all that is and what will be, in a beautiful balance of masculine and feminine from the heart—can you play in the zone of the knowing field. And that is power.

That is Alpha.

SURRENDER IN ACTION

One of the most graceful moments of my life came on a March day in 2008. I was in the NBA minor league, and I had built an incredible body of work. I was ranked the most efficient player per forty-eight minutes in the league, as well as leading the league at the time in double-doubles, where I averaged sixteen points and ten rebounds a game, in twenty-seven minutes. It was the most efficient season of my career. And yet I still had not been called up to the NBA. I felt great frustration and irritation—fear that I was never going to be enough, as a basketball player or as a man. I had done everything I could do and felt like I had hit a glass ceiling and couldn't break through.

It was a Sunday afternoon in Boise, Idaho, when Coach Bryan Gates gathered us on the practice court to talk about how we wanted to finish the season and what were our goals and expectations. We were the best team in the league, having set a recent consecutive win-streak record, and many of us were feeling somewhat burnt out because none of us had been called up to receive an NBA contract while many other players around the league on lesser teams were getting opportunities.

As we went around the group, each one of us articulated what his goals were for the rest of the season and what he wanted to accomplish. When it came time for me to speak, I said, "I realize I haven't been the most present teammate. I have grown frustrated. I have been focusing so hard to get this call-up instead of enjoying my time with you guys and all the things we have accomplished together. I am coming to the truth that if my path does not show me making the NBA, I am truly at a place where I can begin to accept that, because I know I have done everything I could possibly do. No regrets. I know I deserve the call-up, like many of you do, but maybe my lesson in all of this is to see that my worth isn't attached to making the NBA or not. And so, if that is my lesson, to see I am worth more than an NBA job, then I accept it."

I got emotional as I said this to my teammates. I accepted my present situation and I surrendered.

The next day, I was called up to the Cleveland Cavaliers.

There is tremendous power in the feminine energy of surrender. This is not to be abused, thinking we can again twist God's arm into getting our way through false surrender.

The New Alpha male truly surrenders and allows for whatever new developments arrive in the place of a lost dream.

Whether it is a lost game, a failed relationship, money owed to me from teams that never paid, a departed loved one, or a failed business, it is hard for me to let things go. I've had to learn to accept a lot of loss in my life. Many deaths of many dreams.

Yet, the sooner you can accept and surrender to an outcome, the sooner you can allow new and even greater things to come into your life.

I know this is hard to hear, and to trust.

This does not mean it is okay when someone does us wrong. No, we can still hold people accountable with compassionate boundaries and accept reality and let it be what it is.

We were made to let go, to allow new opportunities to come into our lives.

Let things go. Accept the outcome. Let new things come. And find beauty in the detours that seem to take us so far away from our dreams. If you do not accept the detours as they appear when a path has closed, you will become truly lost.

There is sacredness in detours.

It sounds oxymoronic, but looking back on my life at the points where my path deviated from my expected plan, what I thought at first was failure or disappointment, I can see with clarity that not only did those detours take me to interesting places around the world, physically, but more importantly, places inward—emotionally, psychologically, and spiritually—that challenged me, that forced me outside of my comfort zones, to reassess my priorities and my values.

Those deviations from the plan allowed me to empathize with so many people from so many different walks of life. And that is connection, that is intimacy, which I would have never been able to truly experience had my life gone according to *my* plan with ease.

If you are looking at your life, wondering, "Why do I have so many detours and disappointments," you are on the right path. Be grateful for this. The discomfort and eventual acceptance of and surrender to those detours opens the doors for intimacy.

Like the intimacy I found with my teammates on that championship minor league team from Boise, Idaho, who went on to win it all after I signed with the Cavaliers for the rest of the season. That's how good we were as a team. That's how much we trusted each other and had each other's backs. We were bonded together, so much so that when we see each other ten years later, our heart frequencies immediately spin up and conjure the "buzz" we held together in the knowing field that was the sacred space of a basketball court, where we spoke a language that could not be spoken, only felt.

Those detours, spiritual and physical—like the time our bus broke down in the middle of nowhere in North Dakota at two o'clock on a January morning, when we played poker through the night with Sour Patch

Kids as chips to keep our minds off the cold—have created some of the most cherished memories of my life.

Surrendering to sacred detours has taken me all over the world to bond with teammates from all walks of life and cultures, as we chased a dream together. And in that chasing of a dream, we saw each other as our most vulnerable selves, in our deepest fears. In that space, if we were brave enough, we shared compassion, a deep, sacred bond that can never truly be expressed in logic and stat sheets.

Surrender takes us on sacred detours. It creates a space of magic, to let new things come. Surrender requires that we let a dream die. Yes, dreams die—but sometimes they come back. And sometimes they resurrect from the ashes into something far different yet far more powerful than you ever imagined. That is the power of acceptance and surrender—it positions us for transformation.

Do the Work

- » On a piece of paper, write a dream or goal that never came to pass: a career, a relationship, etc. Make it a letter to whoever or whatever you are grieving.
- » Once you are done writing, sign it. Let it sit for the day on the windowsill.
- » At night, when it is dark and the stars are out, take the paper outside and light it with a match. You will transmute the energy of loss, and send it back to the stars, the earth, the universe— whatever energy you ask to take your loss.
- » Do this again the next day and the next day, each time noticing how it is less painful than the time before. There is great power in the healing alchemy of fire.

As you release all those dreams that have died, watching them convert through the flames into the ether, you are creating a space of acceptance, and in that acceptance you are creating space for new things to come. And sometimes those dreams come back, bigger than you ever imagined.

During the grieving process of the divorce, I did this fire alchemy dozens upon dozens of times, sometimes writing a letter to Simon's mother, sometimes to myself, sometimes to Simon, and sometimes to the dream itself that was our marriage.

I cannot emphasize enough the power of this ritual.

It is possibly the greatest gift I am sharing with you in all of this book.

In the Zone

» Take a seat with your back straight against a wall. You may sit cross-legged or with legs straight. For seven minutes, sit with the focused intention of your shoulders being pushed against the wall. Do not let them slouch.

» Begin heart drumming.

» Once you have settled into centeredness, take thirty quick, heavy breaths.

» When you count to thirty, release a slow exhale, noticing the burn in your chest, neck, and shoulders.

» Feel the weight on your shoulders. It will be heavy. You will want to slouch. But you won't. As that weight builds, you will think of all your current stressors, obligations, responsibilities, and duties. All the people who rely on you.

» The weight will become heavier—but you aren't finished.

» Begin to think of all your hopes and dreams that never quite came true. Especially the ones that hurt, that still haunt you with "What if?"

» Let those accumulate.

» After about five minutes, your shoulders and back will be sore and heavy. With all the pressure and weight of expectations and broken dreams, taking a heavy breath will be a struggle, but you can do it.

» Hold it until you can't hold it anymore. (You may begin to cry.)

» Exhale.

» Let your shoulders drop in acceptance and surrender.

» Feel all that weight slip off your shoulders.

» Take as long as you need to gather yourself. When your

breath has calmed, notice the peace in the room. Notice the power of clarity that you wield when you embrace acceptance and surrender.

RECAP

Acceptance gives us clarity in the present moment to make the best decision going forward. It moves us out of the past and the future, into the present where we abide in power. Only then can we take true action. As we continue to accept our place in *what is* with accountability for our contribution to it, we learn that we only control so much, which leads to surrendering to forces greater than ourselves. In that surrender, which again must be earned, there is freedom to let go of old stories and dreams so that we may remain on our path. More importantly, we allow life to work through us, not for us, and especially no longer against us, as we step into true empowerment. It is normal to feel sadness and grief when you step into surrender, as you are now squarely in the energy vortex of death and rebirth, which is the great and powerful catalyst that drives transformation.

(8)

TRANSFORMATION

The Sixth Principle of Perseverance

YOU SIT ON THE WINDOWSILL, wondering if the height is enough to do its job. The last thing you want is to try and do the job and fail at it, spending the rest of your life on a feeding tube.

Your body shakes violently, your breaths are short and shallow. Your tears are hot, salt burning on your skin. So much rage and anger. All those promises you were told—that if you just work hard enough, all your dreams will come true. And you will be happy.

You chased those dreams like the heroes on the movie screen. Yet, once you got to the happy Hollywood ending that said your self-worth would be found, you realized too late how hollow those promises were. All those fair-weather friends and women who loved you when you made the NBA but moved on once you were no longer there. And you hate them, but you also want them to love you again. And you hate yourself for wanting their conditional affection.

Everything is so hollow, so shallow. Even the God you had been told was real is hollow and shallow, not to mention fickle, since he didn't keep his promises.

So much hurt. So much loss. Everything you had toiled and labored for—actual blood, sweat, and tears—gone in an instant, with nothing to show for all the thousands of hours you invested in dark empty gyms, pushing yourself through pain and injury in pursuit of the dream. A dream that said you would find love and validation once you got there.

Nothing to show for it. It's all a joke. This life is just a fluke. And what's the point of even living it?

You are ready for a swan dive, challenging the fates to in fact make you a vegetable. You take your hearing aids out so you can at least die in tranquil silence. You place them on the table right beside the windowsill. And because the table is touching the wall, you feel the vibration of the old clunker phone up the wall into the windowsill. You already know who it is. You don't even have to answer, but you do—the person who first showed you the meaning of accountability.

"Hello, Mom."

DEFINING TRANSFORMATION

"Adapt or die," says the Pluto archetype within us all, the energy of death and rebirth, demanding transformation.

Transformation is the complete evolution of all aspects of who we are—our personality and being, along with the maturation of our values, stories, and fears, as we move into a space of heightened awareness beyond this temporary plane of existence, allowing our true identity to emerge, no longer encumbered by the cultural stories we were told we had to inherit in order to belong.

For me, one was my old gladiator mask, which felt he didn't deserve to laugh in his natural authentic state. Although I was twenty-seven years old when I made the NBA and traveled the world, I still believed my subconscious story that told me I had to earn love, that I had to do something incredible, and only then would God be proud of me. In doing my best to silence those stories, I chased those bright lights of the NBA stage, seeking validation. Through pain, heartache, and more setbacks than I could count, I was finally there in the NBA—a place so many people told me I would never go—where I wasn't allowed to go. And yet, there I was, in the arena under the brightest lights in the world, and I felt no different.

Sure, my ego was happy, but fear was what I felt. I didn't feel I was changed, or saved, or that God loved me more or that he was proud of me. All I felt in my heart was fear—fear that I would fail. I was so rattled when that awareness hit, that the happy Hollywood ending I had chased was a myth.

Fast-forward six months to the fall of 2008—the economy was in a severe recession, and most NBA teams were releasing roster spots or changing out older players for rookies they could sign to minimum contracts to save money.

I was no exception. I was, in fact, expendable.

The morning after the first preseason game the following season, I was released. It was a rainy day in Cleveland. I walked outside into the rain and I remember looking up to the sky, asking the old god I had been raised with, "Where did you go?"

I had done everything I was told to do by my bosses and the front office, by my religious figures, by the movies that promised the happy ending, yet the dream was gone. God had not fulfilled his promise, or at least I told myself that, because in my dualistic, black-and-white programming of God and religion, it meant that either I had done something wrong or that God was a liar. Either/or.

It was in that moment that the god I had been raised with—or better yet the god that someone else told me existed—died.

"God," as I assumed it, fell before my eyes, like the rain.

I had lived twenty-seven years of my life not understanding how to be a leader of my own life, as I attached my worth to the outcomes and stories, some not even my own stories but other people's stories, I'd soaked up like a sponge. With so many clashing agendas, it was impossible to objectively gauge my worth against the outcomes, and yet I did because I had been taught through stories that the next car, next job, next lover, next NBA contract would validate me.

We have all been programmed to consume this. When we attach our worth to the outcomes, we are not being leaders of our own lives; instead, we are aligning our worth with the mercurial opinions of others and their expectations of growth and success. Life, however, is not a linear process of growth. It is sequences and seasons. Things are born. Things die. And they are reborn again in different incarnations. This is the phoenix energy—death and rebirth—and it is a natural and essential pattern in the universe.

When we ask for or expect a consistent and predictable path of linear growth, no matter how attractive that consistency may look, we are asking to plateau. Acceleration is a change of speed and/or direction. Plateauing is the opposite. And yet, many success books and coaches have sold us on the illusion that the plateauing they disguise as consistent growth *is* growth. It is not. Consistent growth is constant and steady acceleration, changing speed and directions through all the detours and obstacles that challenge your comfort zones and perceived truths and stories.

It took me a long time to understand this truth about growth, to understand how to be a leader of my own life. So much of my worth was attached to the outcome as well as the illusion of progress, which I thought to be life working exactly how I expected it to work. In my own logic of growth there was a comfort zone that said if I worked hard enough and pushed myself outside of my comfort zones, I would get a reward, and it would look a certain way. And in that entitlement was a comfort zone.

THE *AHA!* MOMENT

As I recovered from the painful process of a nervous breakdown after my near suicide attempt in Italy, it took me about two years to finally feel grounded, but in a different, more meaningful way. Many friends didn't recognize me anymore. And many of them left my life.

As we grow and transform, we learn to accept the truth that not everyone will come with us. Not all relationships, even the good ones, can come with us.

While I was building a new foundation, I still had many blind spots, and I still do, as enlightenment is an eternal evolution of growth, not some coaching certificate or plaque on a wall. Even after the dream of the NBA ended, I still had an even bigger blind spot waiting to be exposed— the one that said I would someday get married, and then I would *truly* be happy. I was ready to project onto someone else, to play a role, to complete me. I thought that if my wife was perfect and our marriage was perfect, then that would mean I was a good man. Predictably, that came crashing down as well, for no one can be more than human.

Yet, in that deconstruction, in another death of another dream, I found my son—Simon. When I held him for the first time, I finally understood what unconditional love is. Up to that point, it was something I had never allowed myself to feel.

Through my travels around the world, compounded by having my son Simon and being his father, the greatest truth I have learned is this:

Love is either unconditional or it is not love at all.

Anything else is manipulation. If people are withholding love from you to get you to act, speak, or behave a certain way, that is not love, but rather control and, again, manipulation.

With each milestone of Simon's first year, from smiling to sitting up to chattering, I was so proud of the little guy that was my own flesh and blood. One day, near his first birthday, as I was watching him eat Cheerios with his dual appendages—fingers and thumbs—I was fascinated and thought: "How cool!"

I was so proud of him. But then in that moment, I had another thought, an epiphany: "If I can be proud of him, why can't I be proud of myself? Especially the five-year-old boy who had been told that God had made him deaf as a form of punishment?"

I had been ashamed of that five-year-old boy, *me*, with a speech impediment, for years. I wanted to believe he never existed. No. I couldn't be vulnerable or beautifully flawed, an ugly duckling that would in his own perfect time grow into his beautiful adult state.

No, that boy had to be a tough guy, an old alpha. He had to over-compensate and hide behind masks to be somebody else. He had to be cool. He had to earn love. He had to do something nearly impossible, like become the first legally deaf player in NBA history, and then he would be worthy of love and intimacy.

For years I avoided thinking about that five-year-old me. But that is where the hole in my gut came from—the hole screaming for more success and external validation, to hide the pain. It was a void where five-year-old me belonged, but I was not allowing him to rightfully be there. Instead, he was dragging behind, saying, "I am still here! I know you wish you could get rid of me and pretend I never existed, and I wish I could do that, too, but I can't, because I am you and you are me."

In that moment with Simon, I had another thought: If an electron can be in two places at one time, why then can't I—thirty-four-year-old, six-foot-eleven-inch me—walk into that Sunday school room and sit down next to five-year-old me, look him square in the eyes and say, "You are going to do great things. Amazing things. And you are loved. And I am so proud of you."

Can you imagine the look on a little boy's face seeing a man of such large stature walk into the room and validate him? That's all I ever wanted, five-year-old me, for someone to be proud of me, to tell me I was doing a good job. Yet it was up to me the entire time, to heal myself, to take my pain away—to be a leader of my own life. We put unbearable expectations on others to save us.

That was my job, not the NBA's job or my illusory soul mate's.

It was my job to transform my own life. To heal myself. To decide and believe I was enough, perfectly flawed and beautiful in my own place and time.

Five-year-old me didn't need an NBA contract. He didn't need 100,000 Instagram followers. He needed to know that someone had his back.

That I have his back.

And in turn, he has mine.

For I am all stages of me. Infant, toddler, five-year-old, teen, adult me.

My son, the beautiful reflection that he is, taught me how to be a leader of my own life.

SHIFTING VERSUS TRANSFORMING

Transformation calls for not only a complete revolution of your attitude and perspective, but of *everything*. It demands shedding your skin: your stories, cultural identity, biases, and fears.

We are not simply talking about "shifting" and the gentle idiom of "change your thoughts, change your life" here, but rather "change the entire motherboard, change your life."

Shifting is having a change of attitude or perspective while allowing much of your avatar and its cultural identity to remain intact. It's a low wager in hopes of having your life change. Transformation, in contrast, is letting it all—stories, values, beliefs—burn in the refiner's fire, allowing a more natural version of you, your true soul-self, to rise from the ashes and face the world. This is phoenix energy—the energy of death and rebirth. In this painful yet necessary transformation, we learn to redefine our values, stepping into the clarity that we were not born to be caged within our comfort zones of perceived truths, logic, values, expectations, and entitlements. It is being bold enough to check all of them with full accountability and integrity, and accept the truth that those comfort zones are merely illusions.

Transformation is ripping through old scar tissue. It is uncomfortable, sometimes extremely painful. As an athlete, I spent great amounts of time stretching through the distorted scar tissue and trauma I physically suffered in my earlier years. It was constant work, finding old scar tissue and breaking it down, so I could be more flexible and faster as I got older.

As you rip through your own spiritual scar tissue, it allows you to be more flexible, quicker, and more able to let go of other people's drama, abandonment, and projection, as well as no longer weighed down by your own stories as you navigate the world. Transformation is empowering yourself with the accountability of choice, knowing you can, in every moment, choose either clarity of the eternal design or fleeting stories. It is to choose the present with acceptance, or the past and future with resistance. It is to return to stories and bury your head in the sand, or to rise and redefine all of them, carving your own way through life, knowing that when you do become a leader of your own life you can in turn truly lead others.

This is Alpha.

Ask Yourself

» What scar tissue from an old physical wound still limits you?
» What scar tissue from an old emotional wound still limits you?
» We all have trauma to one degree or another. It is an event that causes us to have a fear-based reaction to current or future events. But be honest, how much pain have you brought into your life trying to avoid confronting and healing the *original* pain?
» Is that repetition or transformation?

LEADERSHIP

True leaders not only transform others as they lead, they transform themselves in the process, because if you cannot be a leader of your own life, how can you possibly expect to lead others?

Anyone can read a book on leadership and think they are a leader, but true Alpha leadership is having the courage and grit to redefine it and, more importantly, walk it. Alpha leadership is being able to get yourself entirely out of the way, allowing a greater force to operate through you, no longer needing recognition because you know fleeting praise is simply that—fleeting. So many people want to be leaders for the praise, but so few are willing to do the work of transformation, helping us all move into a space of trust and empowerment, no longer one of scarcity and reaction.

Transforming into a leader of your own life is the accountability that you have far more choice—not control but choice—in this life than you might be comfortable with: you can react and resist, or accept and respond.

It was my choice, every time, to respond with clarity or react with fear whenever someone got in my way—on the basketball court and in life. It was my choice to get up every time I got knocked down. Always my choice. It was my choice to allow my worth to be attached to the illusions of worth the world has sold us. It was my choice to adopt the values and logic of those around me, believing them to be truth.

It has always been my choice.

Transforming into the leader of my life means choosing, with each thought, to question every thought—is this Lance thinking, or is it my culture of polygamist thought patterns thinking? Are these thoughts even mine? Are these values mine? Or are they values I am adopting to fit in, to belong, for fear of abandonment?

If I am adopting someone else's values to belong, I am choosing to play a role. Instead, I choose to empower myself with the accountability of choice: that it is my choice every day to detach my worth from the outcome, knowing that the truth is never as good as it seems or as bad as it seems. With accountability, and always seeking growth, you know that "failing" is simply stepping outside of your comfort zones, knowing that is where growth is found.

Transforming into a leader is knowing that if you are not experiencing failure you are failing at life.

Transforming into a leader of your life is not only no longer attaching your worth to all the drama but boldly keeping your own beat through it all. While everyone else is riding the roller coaster of madness, attaching their worth to the highs and the lows, you choose to march to your own beat of integrity, unafraid of other people's fear-based projections and fickle abandonment.

This is your worth: the beat you keep through it all. When you are able to do this, you become truly fearless, knowing your worth is never in question, knowing that you can step outside your comfort zone and fail, and with accountability, pick yourself up and keep playing on, knowing you are only learning and growing as you continually venture into the unknown.

As you challenge the unknown, transforming and blazing your own trail of internal leadership, you will experience so many deaths of so many dreams. And with each death of a dream you see yet another illusion crumble, an illusion that once told you that you are separate, that you are not enough, that you need more, to be whole.

> A truly transformed Alpha male is one who is brave enough and bold enough to write his own criteria as he discovers his true soul-self, while leading others to do the same.

With each death of a dream another line of clarity is extended to you, to help you see that you are not separate from but rather an extension of Creation.

With each death of a dream you see the roles we all play, and how those roles no longer serve you, and how many others will in fact abandon you when you no longer wish to play those roles—and this a good thing, for it is far better to be on your journey alone than to be surrounded by those who doubt your path, unable to "see" you in your authentic state.

With each death of a dream you see that your worth could never be in question, that you are never truly alone on your journey, for all roads lead back to Creation.

And with that clarity, you continue to get up each morning, with a full heart, never afraid. That is leadership.

Why do we keep fighting the good fight through these illusions? Why do we keep getting back up every time we get knocked down?

Because we choose to, understanding that clarity is the ultimate reward. Clarity that our worth is not attached to an outcome, to the superficial and mercurial standards of success dictated by family, tribe, culture, or society. It is understanding your worth that is far greater than the criteria of what the egoic collective conscience of fear around you dictates.

Transforming into a New Alpha male, a true leader, means not only challenging the unknown but embracing it by being willing to walk the uncharted planes where few dare to venture, into the realms of no-*thing*. Where nothing is everything. And one is all. Where all dimensions are inextricably linked as a holographic whole. A truly transformed Alpha male is one who is brave enough and bold enough to write his own criteria as he discovers his true soul-self, while leading others to do the same.

Extending that clarity to others is leadership.

This is Alpha.

SERVICE AND ABUNDANCE

The evolution of the New Alpha male is a complete transformation of all values, even his perspective on money and scarcity.

The old alpha male would say something like this: "I take care of myself first because I am tired of people always taking from me."

I hear this or something comparable quite often. It is time to transform and reframe this short-sighted "me first" platitude.

I could walk into any new team's locker room and within five minutes know who the "team-first" givers were and who were the takers. I was a natural giver, and as such, I expected everyone to have the same standard of giving and team-first mentality. I was continually disappointed—such is the world of paradoxical scarcity that is professional team sports. I had a choice many times to stem that part of my soul that wanted to give, for fear that others would take advantage of it. I checked myself and transformed the narrative with two truths:

1. If I am giving with the expectation to get something back, it is not a true give, but rather an attempted manipulation, a control tactic.
2. Instead of choosing to no longer be a giver or of service, I choose to be accountable and spend more time researching and discerning who I am giving to or partnering with, rather than blaming the act of giving itself.

Givers are the most unsuccessful, and conversely, the most successful people in the world. Not to mention the happiest. The trick is in learning to surround yourself with other givers. That is how you make sure you are on the winning side of giving, and not the martyr side. Embedding yourself with other givers is the key to being as effective as possible in your desire to give and be of service.

The ability to be of service to others is true abundance and wealth, because it can never be taken away from you. Even in the lowest points of your life, you don't need money to serve others. It doesn't cost you a dollar to help someone cross a street or to pick up a shovel and help another dig a trench. That is limitless, it is infinite, and thus it is true abundance.

The ability to serve, to give of my time, like walking into a deaf school and seeing the students' faces light up, makes me feel like the wealthiest man in the world. Far wealthier than my paychecks or standing underneath the bright lights of professional basketball arenas.

True abundance gives you joy. Yes, money makes you comfortable, and utilized correctly, money empowers you to help and empower others. Money, if used well, amplifies the limitless abundance to serve. But does money itself give you joy? No. However, it might amplify your ability to experience many things that give you joy.

While we are here on the issue of wealth, let's talk about money. I grew up in a culture where money was shamed, especially by those at the top who freely took from the community coffers but didn't want the rest of us to get any ideas. We were raised to be uncomfortable with even talking about money, because the love of money was evil. My discomfort with talking about money plagued me until my mid-thirties. Heaps of money would come into my bank account, and then it would disappear.

And it wasn't like I was buying new cars and boats or going out clubbing. It was from failed real-estate attempts and other endeavors I believed were sound.

One day while in the midst of a heavy week-long meditation theme of working my way around the energy of money, I had an epiphany: for all of my life up to that point, I had equated money with female energy. Just as I had been shy and uncomfortable around women, feeling like I had to earn their love, I carried the same story with money: I had to earn it in fear, as though I didn't naturally deserve it. Because, like women, money will always choose the best man, or so the old story said.

Once I recognized that narrative of money being equated with female energy, I began to allow the energy around money to move to the center, no longer so predominantly feminine. I began transforming and reframing my dynamic in the way I behave with my best friends, which is:

I don't always see my friends. They come and go in my life, but I know whenever I need them, they will always have my back. They will be there. And I will have their backs as well. They know I will always love them and will be grateful for whatever time I get with them.

This.

This simple transformation around the energy of money jumpstarted the entire flow and stability of money into my life, and, more importantly, the flow of abundance into my life—the ability and opportunities to serve others. To empower my voice to reach more people and to be of service to them in empowering them to find their true voices, to be the leaders of their own lives, by reframing their own stories that no longer serve them.

This was all it took. After years of trying all the self-help books about finances, this simple transformation around the energy of money changed it all for me.

I am now a wealthy man.

Not because of money, but because wealth and abundance are the ability to serve others.

We see a lot of posturing on social media about "success," but success without paying it forward is not wealth, but rather scarcity. We have all been burned at one time or another when we tried to do something genuinely kind to someone and they took it for granted or threw it in our face. It hurts, trying to open a vein of intimate connection with someone by being of service to them, and yet they reject it. It is a different type of embarrassment than a romantic rejection. And it leaves a horrible taste in your mouth.

However, that taste in your mouth prompts a good question: were you giving altruistically, or were you giving as a manipulation tactic to receive a certain desired reaction, prompting your own dopamine boost?

Success without paying it forward is not wealth, but rather scarcity.

As you work through those old societal control mechanisms you will find yourself giving more freely, knowing if people don't appreciate it, it has no bearing on your worth and your heart. Just because people struggle to be vulnerable and fail to tell you how much your kindness means to them, don't ever for a second feel that service is useless.

Kindness matters. You never know who will be watching or paying attention. Whenever I speak to educators or school administrators, I tell a story about Mrs. Ogden, my sixth-grade teacher. As a twelve-year-old, I was still a part of the Allred group at the time, and with my hearing and speech issues, I dealt with a lot of bullying and was angry. I pushed back pretty hard, taking it out on my teachers. Many teachers had struggled with me through elementary school, but it was Mrs. Ogden who finally broke through.

I remember it being a rough time; I had been acting out in defiance.

Mrs. Ogden took one minute out of her day and 10 percent more of her heart when she sat me down, while everyone was out to recess, and said, "Lance, I am beginning to understand that with your hearing loss, your brain has been forced to adapt and see the world in a different way. And many people are going to struggle with your different lens and perspective. They might even label you as rude, stubborn, and arrogant."

Then she said, "And promise me that you will never conform."

This was in 1993.

In that one minute, Mrs. Ogden helped position me on the path of lifelong transformation by telling me in so many words to boldly grow and experience life at my own natural evolution and pace, and not as the world would dictate. Furthermore, she was planting a seed within me to learn to self-love. And though self-love would be the hardest lesson I would ever learn in life, the transformation that was required was necessary for me to truly step into my full size, a giant, with an even bigger heart, no longer shrinking his size to fit in or apologizing for it.

In August of 2018, while I was speaking to educators in central Utah, I shared that story of Mrs. Ogden to let them know that even if their students don't say thank you, those little acts matter. Unbeknownst to me, Mrs. Ogden was quietly sitting in the crowd. She came up to me after I was done speaking and was signing books. When I saw her, I began to weep. And she did as well. In that moment, Mrs. Ogden was the wealthiest woman in the world. She was rewarded with the abundance of knowing that her time and service and, furthermore, her kindness and compassion mattered. It had clarified a lifelong legacy for her—a legacy that emboldened a kid like me to be prepared for a world of backlash and criticism, and to never back down. And all of her peers, teachers and administrators, standing in line that day got to witness the truth as well: that their service matters.

To all my friends in education, social work, or any social services where you sometimes feel what you do doesn't matter, I promise you it does. And to anyone who wishes to give of their heart and time in service to others, the promise holds true for you as well.

Whereas the old alpha male hoards his money in scarcity as a social status marker, fearing everyone wants to take it from him, the New Alpha male understands that abundance comes in many forms and is limitless. When we have transformed to align with the limitless energy of abundance, no longer separate from it, we can truly be of service to others, able to give more authentically, altruistically, and efficiently. The New Alpha male understands that wealth is service. And service is leadership.

Even if you are not walking around with loads of cash, you can still be wealthier than the richest man in the world by finding the joy that is the human connection and intimate bonding of spirits through the sacred act of service. This is true abundance. Go dance with it.

This is Alpha.

MARKETED EXPECTATIONS

The New Alpha male in a state of transformation is willing to be in a place of discomfort long enough to decide for himself what is best for his own path, not what advertisements or social media tell him. He knows that whether he has a million followers, one, or none, his worth and value as a human being does not change. He doesn't suffer from FOMO: Fear of Missing Out.

He actually has JOMO: Joy of Missing Out.

Social media has created the illusion of instant gratification, instant success, all the while staying within your filtered comfort zones. Funny thing about social media, though: it's an illusion, just like comfort zones are illusions.

I didn't have an active Twitter or Instagram account until after I retired from basketball, as I preferred my privacy. It would blow your mind how many times I would sit in a pro locker room and watch a teammate literally *buy* likes and *buy* followers for their social media posts.

Illusions.

If you look at most influencers online, I would wager a strong chance that most of their followers were bought, especially "influencers" who haven't accomplished anything. This is a bet I would take anytime, against any influencer, because I get solicited every day online by people trying to sell me more likes, comments, and followers to boost my ranking. I am a prime target for these account boosters' services as I am in the public speaker domain and thus, according to their numbers, a likely consumer for "padding my stats" to show potential clients how important I am.

And it is tempting.

When we get stuck in the social media warp, we are conditioned to feel "never enough." And we keep going back, because it is an addiction. Validation addiction. My addiction.

And the addiction to instant gratification.

Which is not the real world.

While social media has been helpful for me as a marketing tool and a way to keep in touch and keep track of friends, I myself have fallen into the trap of it somehow being a sounding board for my value and my message. This is a false narrative. I have to check this narrative every day, because the competitor, the athlete within me, wants to take a lot of these other influencers down—influencers who sell dreams and happily-ever-afters.

It's all a game. A game of selling celebrity, which is one of America's greatest exports in our current global economy. It's a game of selling a myth that your worth is outside yourself, a game where people hope if they take enough selfies with celebrities, they will be viewed as successful influencers and thought leaders.

Although I frown upon the trend of people self-labeling, I will be a "thought leader" for a moment and ask some questions: How often have you checked on "influencers" who are selling success, to see what price they paid to be where they are on stage talking to you about said success? What did they actually accomplish before they became a guru? Did they truly walk the walk before they started the talk and give themselves abstract labels like "influencer," which cannot be measured with clear criteria and so can never truly be contested? Let's use an example. I will now label myself a "literary luminary." Good luck tearing that fancy certificate down off my wall—it's subjective.

Social media has its graces, but again, do not buy into the game that it is somehow a true reflection of your worth and value. That is the machine wanting us to feel incomplete, thus primed to consume as we begin to look outside of ourselves for happiness. Have the courage to transform or even revert back and place social media where it belongs— as a fun way to engage with your friends or market your business if you are an entrepreneur, but do not buy into the illusions of happiness and FOMO that so many "influencers" are selling.

People are not nearly as happy or successful as they position themselves to be on social media—this I guarantee. How do I know? Because when you get to peek or even live behind the curtain of the NBA marketing machine, arguably one of the best marketing machines in the world, you see the truth behind the illusion, which is fear and lack: scarcity.

Whenever you start to feel a twinge of jealousy, or FOMO, do yourself a kindness and remember that Christmas present you were so excited to get as a kid, and then remember how quickly the excitement wore off.

The New Alpha male is courageous enough to detach from the feeding tube that is social media, able to live in the discomfort that he does not need to know all the trends, because that is what they simply are—trends.

Instead of FOMO, the New Alpha male relishes JOMO, a wonderful form of self-care, as he transforms into a true influencer, a self-influencer, by being enough for and of himself, whether he has 100,000 followers or none at all.

This is Alpha.

FAMILY

In the process of transformation, the New Alpha male asks: What is family?

He begins to see and understand family as much more than a group of people sharing the same blood for a lifetime and then dying. On a deeper level, he begins to know and feel in his bones the truth of epigenetics—the processes that alter gene activity without changing the DNA sequence, like family trauma and legacies—and that we are primely positioned to help redirect family DNA patterns of trauma, shame, and loss.

What does this look like?

It manifests as possessing the presence and self-awareness to catch the patterns of behavior that have plagued your family lineage for generations: poverty, shame, guilt, abuse, trauma, denial, and other patterns that are detrimental to the expansion of consciousness.

You know you have found one when you notice yourself judging and speaking negatively of an ancestor and are also in enough awareness to recognize you are likely projecting and exhibiting (at least to some degree) a portion of the underlying energy and story that prompts (or prompted) the behavior in need of healing. Once you see the behavior and pattern, you consciously sit with it, breathe with it, allow yourself to feel it, and in deep meditation, transmute it, acknowledging the energy for the purpose it served for a time in your family line to cope with fear of or actual abandonment. That coping mechanism may have helped for a while, to allow your family to adapt to a new reality, and you can honor it in that way.

We can go deeper and talk about physical or sexual abuse. Somewhere in a family line, disempowerment and scarcity led to shame. That shame was perpetuated to the point where it manifested in a vicious and heinous grab to possess some power, even if it meant hurting and abusing a loved one. Future generations continued the behavior or manifested the shame in similar or different acts, but with shame being the underlying pattern haunting the family line. This is not to say that acts of violence and abuse toward others are okay. It is, however, allowing compassion to come into the picture, to create the space for the shame, humiliation, and fear of abandonment to transmute and move.

A New Alpha male takes his own painful, raw experiences and transforms them into teaching points to help heal others. He knows how to do the same for his family line, by honoring them but stopping the patterns. It is important to pay respect to our ancestors and bloodline, even if we don't particularly like everyone in it. Denying our ancestors is a form of self-loathing. As we release our pain, our ancestors need us to surrender the family baggage and return it to them, where they can transmute and transform it.

New Alphas can begin to heal energy and transmute the wounding of their family line, and with honor send it back to the source, allowing their ancestors to do their part in healing the DNA trauma. In our hubris, even if we do honor our ancestors, we often do so in a patronizing way, as though they were simple people, like pets, and they couldn't possibly be as smart and wise are we are now with all the technology and data at our fingertips. This is nonsense. Not only was their threshold for discomfort higher than ours, but our ancestors had fewer distractions preventing them from their human experience and the emotions and feelings that come with it. They may be wiser than us, as they continue to work in the interdimensional planes, having already experienced this earthly journey. Our parents and ancestors do not need us to save them; they need us to break patterns of trauma.

Many of our fears are not solely ours but are linked to our family DNA. It takes healing the entire family line to fully heal a wound. Send it back to your ancestors, to those family constellations shining through eternal spheres. This is healing the family line. Nobody needs a super-man who wants to do it all by themselves. Furthermore, that is the antithesis of the entire point of family.

We do it together.

A specific wounding and pattern pertaining to my paternal line that needs healing is martyrdom. Not only was my grandfather a literal martyr, killed for his religious beliefs, but his father, my great-grandfather, gave up a seat as a senator from Idaho to begrudgingly honor a church calling. His bitterness was journaled and recorded—instilling the belief that religion requires the sacrifice of not just happiness but your entire life. I would not be surprised if his father had a similar energy, but that is not my job to know, nor do I need to know. I do know enough to see the pattern of martyrdom and my own behaviors and replication of the underlying energy of it and how martyrdom manifested in my life in patterns of loss and duty, with happiness somehow being considered selfish. Instead of passing that pattern on to my son, it is my job to transmute it without judgment and send it back up the line.

It is my job to see the pattern of martyrdom and give it compassion and understanding for the way martyrdom was a coping mechanism spun up by the human brain in its attempt to explain why bad things happen when you are living and working so hard to have a good life. That logic served its purpose for a time, but it no longer serves me or my family line. I honor my family line by seeing the pattern, acknowledg-ing it, accepting it, and forgiving it with compassionate understanding. This releases the curse, so to speak, and primes it to transmute. I can send it back up the family line, to let my ancestors do their work on their end, wherever they may be, as our energetic bond transcends the limited frequencies of this three-dimensional experience on Earth.

I work for this transformation not only on behalf of myself, but for the entire family line.

My father contributed his own crucial part in transforming family patterns by being a much more involved father than his own father (which wasn't hard to do as my father was one of forty-eight children, and thus his father couldn't really be that involved), establishing a dynamic for us to connect more deeply and authentically, able to evolve together as we grew. For example, I was the youngest of my father's eight children and I was also the only child whose diapers he changed. He had grown up in a world where his mother reprimanded and chastised him for even trying to change my oldest sister's diaper, for that was beneath the man, the patriarch. However, my size and strength were too much for my mother to handle by the time I was ten months old, so my father took pity on her after I gave her a good kick in the face and stepped in to finish the diaper change. From there, my father and I had a bond.

As my father began to watch over me and my development, I know his own emotional development transformed. By being willing to cross the gender role divide and deign to change his own child's diapers, a metamorphosis was set in motion that saw my father emerge from being a macho man to a much more rounded man who showed me through action the power and necessity of being cerebral. Although my father wasn't a basketball player, his ability to evolve and be multifaceted was the greatest act of mentorship during my basketball career.

> The son heals the father by allowing the father the opportunity to see his reflection and grow into integrity.

This transformative transcendence was triggered for me as well when my son, Simon, was born. I was thirty-three years old. I felt I was ready to be a father, but I had no idea the impact my son would have on me. Following my father's example, I changed Simon's diapers right away, despite my hair-trigger gag reflex. While I don't miss changing the diapers, I appreciate the bond it gave us. It is pure vulnerability and trust. And love. It was transformational in showing me what unconditional love truly is.

It was me in a state of complete power, giving grace, kindness, and love to a vulnerable being, with no strings attached.

The son heals the father by allowing the father the opportunity to see his reflection and grow into integrity.

When we understand that men who pose as tough guys are terrified to behave in such loving and vulnerable ways because they don't know how to process such intimacy, because likely they never received it in their early development, we are Alpha. Many males have been conditioned to be afraid of pure basic intimacy, as though it signals we are weak, and others will exploit it. My father was raised to be afraid of intimacy, but he broke his cultural and family chain with me. While I already admired him, I didn't understand how much so, until I became a father myself.

Just as my father grew with me, my own emotional intelligence has grown being a father. In learning to help Simon breathe through his emotions, I have taught myself to do the same. In learning to help Simon define his feelings, I have taught myself to do the same and not be ashamed of them. In learning to help Simon be bold and brave, unafraid to fail, I only reaffirm the same for myself whenever I feel fear come into my life. In learning to help Simon understand that his worth and value are never attached to an outcome, I have seen that same clarity for myself as a single father in the hardest times of my life.

Becoming a parent or mentor is possibly the most powerful opportunity to heal, not only yourself but the generations before you. Having a child, blood or not, is a beautiful mirror to reflect back to you your own internal dialogue and self-value. It is one of the greatest gifts we can receive. Yet, most of us do not see it so clearly. Some days we see it as a burden that we have this annoying, whiny kid, always clinging to us. When you understand your child is your mirror, you see with clarity that when you are annoyed with your child, you are annoyed with yourself. If you don't like your child that day, most likely you don't like yourself or your life either. If someone physically or emotionally abuses their child, the simple truth is they cannot stand the sight of their own self, and their child is simply that: their reflection and a target to receive their own projection of self-loathing. When a narcissist rejects bonding with their child, they are devoid of true intimacy with themselves.

When you are at peace with your life and who you are as an eternal, spiritual being, you find the same peace when you look at your child. Simple mirrors. When you see your reflection in those mirrors, you know you are transforming. All relationships are mirrors to help us learn about ourselves, with none starker than the mirror that is your child. When you see your child with gratitude, understanding the perfect opportunity they are giving you to heal yourself with compassion and accountability, you heal not only yourself but them and, furthermore, your ancestors. You heal the line.

The son heals the father, by allowing the father the opportunity to see his reflection and grow into integrity. This is not to say that every day as a single father I am moving with such clarity. Absolutely not.

Honoring evolutionary biology, I don't think men are necessarily coded to hang out with toddlers for twelve straight hours. It has been a grueling challenge for me and my patience. At the height of my stress and fear in my transition, there were some days I was ready to jump in a car and drive toward the sunset—after I put Simon to bed, freshly bathed and pampered, of course.

Thank God for playdates.

Simon continually pulls me out of my head and into the present, when oftentimes all I want to do is be in my head. He continually pushes me out of my comfort zones. He continually challenges my patience and compassion. In learning to help a four-year-old boy own his feelings, I was forced to do the most uncomfortable thing of my life: face my own. Being a father to Simon taught me one of the most powerful skills of the New Alpha male: the transformative power of vulnerability.

Old alpha males enforce traditional gender roles in the home, where the daughters play the role of princess and the sons are told to "toughen up" at the first sign of feelings. For boys are not supposed to talk about feelings, but rather fix them and/or suppress them. If they don't, they will be wounded or abandoned. The New Alpha male is a father and mentor who teaches his children the value of hard work, accountability, and integrity, fusing those principles with vulnerability and authenticity.

It is about showing his children that stale, old societal gender roles empower no one to ascend into their true authentic space. It is transforming into a teacher to help his children learn the power of the blending of masculine and feminine energies, and the internal balance that comes from such a discipline—which is the gateway to intimacy, with yourself and others.

It is about knowing more about dinosaurs than paleontology professors do, because you have a four-year-old kid.

It is about being a superhero at a moment's notice when you drop your kid off at school only to realize, due to a computer glitch in the schedule, that it is your day for parent volunteering in the kindergarten class. You step up to the plate like a badass to play Johnny Appleseed without batting an eye, giving those kids a hell of a show while serving them the best damned apple juice and applesauce they will ever taste in their lives, not because it is homemade—it's not—but because you served it like a beast who doesn't apologize for his dad game being lit.

It is about understanding that your child's sense of self-worth will grow stronger in correlation to the amount of quality time you spend with your child, which is also spending time with yourself. It is about living in the beautiful dichotomy of love and exhaustion, where you can't wait for your son to go back to his mother for a night so you can catch a breather, but then you miss him like hell as soon as he is gone.

New Alpha male fatherhood is the transformation of learning to laugh and appreciate the simple things in life again, such as watching a video about the planets with your four-year-old boy who laughs mischievously when he says, "Venus sounds like penis."

It is about waking up in the middle of the night from a nightmare in which you were drowning, only to realize someone had indeed vomited a chocolate milk corndog smoothie all over you. And with tired eyes, but a grateful heart that you can be there for him, you eagerly change the bed and bathe your boy, wishing you could take all of his pain away. And yet you know you can't, and that life will only give him much worse. And all you can do is be there for him, where you constantly help him to know and never forget that his big, bold heart is the most important and beautiful thing in the world.

The New Alpha male is not threatened by his children outgrowing or outshining him. Rather, he passes all of his wisdom freely, empowering them to be leaders of their own lives and leaders to others, for his legacy is their legacy, as their legacy is his all the way down the family line.

The New Alpha male loves his children unconditionally, with no strings attached, with no manipulation, and emboldens his children to love others and themselves as bravely.

He understands his children have as much to teach him as he does them, as we all collectively heal and evolve into higher beings.

Thank you, sweet Simon.

Do the Work

Transformation is seeing all the reflections, illusions, and stories around you, no longer attaching your worth to them, able to look in the mirrors without fear, taking the subtle truths and lessons they have to teach and then releasing the rest.

ONE

Face the trauma head on. Go into that memory and let the younger version of you know the truth beyond their limited lens, which is that they are deserving of love. Let them see and heal through a different lens, your current lens. No longer let the lens through which they experienced their trauma, often a child or victim lens, be the lens through which you continue to go through your life. Give them a new lens, and they will give you a new lens as well. Spend a week with each person in you who is stuck in a place of trauma or hell. Help them heal. Help yourself heal. Be a leader of your own life.

Learn to use the word "choose" more in your vocabulary. It will make many people uncomfortable, because we aren't conditioned to absorb such brash control of our lives. Less "I have to; I need to." More "I choose to."

I choose to go the store tonight.

I choose to wake up at 5:00 a.m. for an early start at work.

I choose to empower myself to be a leader of my own life.

It sounds trite, but it isn't. It is uncomfortable, bringing in the Principle of Discomfort. And you can apply that homework to this.

Also, every day you will find an old story within your psyche that you still operate under, a story that enables too many assumptions and perceived truths that no longer serve you, and you will write it down.

"I am not handsome enough to be successful."

Next to it, you will write a new truth:

"I am handsome enough to be successful because I choose to."

We have hundreds of bugs and glitches in our psyche and mental coding.

This will become a daily practice, of finding an old truth and updating your brain's hard drive without batting an eye, like you would your smartphone.

TWO

» Be brave in finding and facing down a destructive family pattern.
» Call it out.
» Find the fear at its root and see how it became entangled with your family line.
» Give it compassion, even admiration for how it served your family for a time in dealing with trauma.
» Transmute it by acknowledging it, releasing it, and sending it back up the line.
» Transform the energy of whatever fear is behind it into gratitude for the new appreciation and understanding you will have for your family.

In the Zone

» Sit cross-legged and begin heart drumming until you reach Theta.
» Put your hands in prayer position pushed together at your chest.
» Once you have found relaxation and presence you will bring your hands together again, in prayer pose over your heart.
» With each breath, you will begin breathing like a snore, utilizing the uvula in the back of your mouth and triggering the vagus nerve in your throat. In and out, you will breathe like you are snoring. This will stimulate deep calm and relaxation in your brain.
» Once you feel calm and centered, you will focus on *one* story. It can be one you have been wanting to address for a while.

Or it can be one that suddenly pops up, unexpectedly, from a dark recess you have never noticed before.

» Consciously breathing, you will look at the story and imagine it as an object or a painting, resting on the beach. With each breath, you are the ocean tide, in and out. Watch the water flow over the painting, dissolving the paint. Notice which colors are the first to go, then the subsequent colors until the canvas is blank.

» On that empty canvas, you will choose to paint something new. Your subconscious will know. Let the tide continue to cascade, with each trip casting a color over the canvas. What image is your mind painting on the canvas? How are you painting a new story? This image will be the replacement etched in your mind that will step in whenever your old story wants to reemerge. This image will be its replacement, forever.

» When you are done with the image, continue to breathe normally. Keeping your palms pressed together, raise them to the sky above your head while taking a long slow inhale, and breathe for twenty seconds. Release and open your eyes.

» Do your best to physically draw, paint, or sketch the painting your subconscious made from the transmuted story that no longer serves you. Put that image somewhere you can see it every day, as a reminder of a story that once was but no longer is, and a reminder of the choice you made to transform your life.

RECAP

Transformation is leadership, not just externally—the culture and those around you in your home or workplace—but within yourself.

True transformation is learning to be a leader of your own life.

It is the clarity that your worth is not attached to an outcome, or to the superficial and mercurial standards of success dictated by your family, tribe, culture, or societal upbringing. It is seeing your worth as something far greater than the criteria of what the egoic collective conscience of fear around you dictates.

It is choosing to write your own criteria.

It is understanding that your own life experiences provide for you your own formula on how to navigate this life, as a leader of your own life.

It is the clarity that you are responsible for your own healing and validation.

This is Alpha.

WINNING

9

FORGIVENESS AND GRATITUDE

The Seventh Principle of Perseverance

IN THE POSTGAME QUIET of a locker room, once the rumble and murmurs of the crowd have faded from the arena, after you have looked at the stat sheet too many times, trying to logically make sense of what just happened, you find a place of reflection.

A place of introspection, where you are able to look back through your own eyes with clarity and see how and why the game unfolded as it did. And this clarity does not come from stat sheets; it comes from your own inner knowing, if you dare to sit with yourself long enough to see it.

DEFINING FORGIVENESS AND GRATITUDE

Forgiveness pairs with gratitude—they cannot be one without the other and are the highest vibrational frequency upon which we can operate as humans. Forgiveness and gratitude are the final stage of full transformation, and thus the last of the Seven Principles of Perseverance. True perseverance, true grit, is choosing to be brave enough to forgive and also hold gratitude for our painful experiences while simultaneously knowing that while they don't always happen for a reason, we can give them meaning by choosing to find the lesson in the experience.

Forgiveness has become stagnant in the realm of victimization in our litigious and enabling world of social media and 24/7 news. This is not to say that people aren't victimized by awful actions, but this has been diminished because the notion of forgiveness has been hamstrung in a world where people with entitlement seek to feel wronged. When we are told "Forgive others, not for them but for yourself," it is still holding onto a sad story that you were wronged and you are a victim. Stories are important—they are how we share messages and experiences for others to relate to us and learn. A story is a perspective, and we choose how we narrate it. Are they self-absorbed stories that seek attention and pity, draining and taking from others? Or are they empowering stories that are gifts that you share with others to make their paths easier? Do you tell your stories with abundance or with lack? As a teacher or as a victim?

When it comes to forgiveness and gratitude, the New Alpha transforms his stories into empowering lessons, not only to truly release the wrongs committed against him, but because, if he is brave enough, he also finds gratitude for those experiences. This is why I believe gratitude and forgiveness—and I mean *true* forgiveness—go hand in hand.

BALANCING DARK AND LIGHT

This is not to say we are grateful for hurtful actions performed against us; they can be painful and traumatic. Would I want to experience many of life's hard lessons again? Hell no, but as you work through that suffering, try what I call "dark and light balance work." Breathe and hold a space for the wrongs and pain in one hand, while bravely holding gratitude in the other hand. In one hand you can feel misery and anger, and in the other hand you can choose to hold thankfulness, seeing from the eye of higher consciousness, from the greater whole, the valuable lessons of clarity those experiences give to you in regard to your worth as you find the balance of both—grief and gratitude—in your center, your heart. Honor your feelings each time, neither downplaying nor shaming them, for you are human, and what makes us human is our ability to feel. When we can hold the space of dark and light, grief and gratitude at the same time, we have become centered in our hearts, owning the dynamic ability of the human to embrace and honor multiple emotions at once, with grace and power—in balance—for balance is power.

As I look back, some days the clouds are heavy, and it takes work to rise through trauma. We all have those days, but you remind yourself that those clouds are simply that—passing clouds. As you work and breathe through them, practicing every day like you would your free-throw shots, those clouds become less overwhelming. With those clear skies of clarity comes gratitude. So much gratitude for our experiences, even the painful ones, which allow and sometimes force us to peel away our masks and reveal our eternal, immeasurable worth as we navigate our journey through the stars.

For me, there's gratitude for my Sunday school teacher who impressed upon me that God had made me deaf as a form of punishment, not only showing me what unconditional love is *not*, but setting me on a path of discovery to find out how much I am truly loved—unconditionally, eternally. Gratitude to my Allred relatives who sued and disowned my family, again, for showing me what unconditional love is not.

There's gratitude for Coach Majerus, who showed me the price of integrity and the path I had to take to hold it, and, furthermore, for showing me the price my parents paid in their path of integrity. Gratitude to all the basketball fans across the world who projected their hatred onto me in those fleeting moments of competition, for showing me that the true ills of the world are not the superficial symptoms of violence, pornography, drugs, and alcohol, but rather fear. Gratitude to all those teams that never paid me, showing me yet again the fear within which most of us operate and the mentality of lack that drives so much of our world, blocking trust and intimacy. Gratitude to the collapse of my NBA dream, allowing me to peek behind the curtain, revealing that my worth cannot be found under the brightest lights in an arena, but rather in the quiet moments when I am one with myself, staring at stars, seeing I am endless, limitless, and here for but a moment to help others and even the universe know a little bit more about our own humanity and divinity.

Gratitude to the mother of my son, for she is the only person I could have loved so madly to get me to take those first steps of vulnerability, which exposed so many more subconscious beliefs, blind spots, and cultural coding limiting my human experience. Beliefs telling me my worth as a man was contingent on who validated me in a relationship. I never would have seen these blind spots if it had not been for her. In my longing for her to complete me, I learned to complete myself. And I am grateful to her. On one hand, I still hold sadness over the loss of our marriage, and on the other, I hold gratitude.

True forgiveness is gratitude.

It is not easy. It takes tremendous courage. It takes a New Alpha.

Learning to find and move into this gratitude with accountability, as a male from this culture with the many wounds that triggered me to recoil at intimacy and love, was harder than making the NBA.

I mean that.

It was extremely difficult learning to be not only more mindful of my triggers and fears but more *heartful*, meaning we as humans can feel all the pain and loss of life while at the same time hold gratitude for it as we see the bigger picture, gracefully balancing the dark and the light.

Only true spiritual gladiators can do this—those who are bold and brave enough to show all their scars and wounds, and to not feel shame, but rather smile with gratitude at the beauty of those scars, for they are the timeline of your grit, the symbols of your perseverance on the path you have walked in your journey into the heart. A fully realized heart can never be defeated or destroyed, as it is a vortex, a stargate to the worlds beyond.

The sword I now wield is gratitude. And that gratitude is so strong, so bright, that some days it hurts. In that gratitude, I know that there will be many more wounds, even deaths I will experience, and with each one will come *more* clarity and even more gratitude. I welcome it, for I know it will only make my heart bolder and more fearless as it guides my journey.

PICTURES OF YOU

Boxes, so many boxes. I lost many things when I retired from basketball—a happy home, a beautiful marriage. What little I could take with me was packed away. All I had to show for a ten-year professional basketball career were my possessions packed away in storage. I clung to those boxes during the last two years of living in my transitory basement apartment, my cocoon.

One day I will open them, I told myself.

Yet, here I am once again, transitioning and downsizing to an even smaller space, aiming to own a modest duplex, which means what can't fit into my new space has to go—half of my possessions, half of my boxes.

So many boxes of so many somedays: *Someday I will compose that song on my keyboard. Someday I will paint that picture I've envisioned on that empty canvas. Someday I will lay out that train set for me and Simon. Someday I will unpack all my jerseys and frame them.* As we know, someday often never comes, and those boxes are never opened.

As I withdraw photos from picture frames, stacking said frames in a box to donate, I stumble upon a box with an NBA jersey inside that I said I would someday put in a shadowbox. But I wonder if it is worth the effort anymore. Underneath that jersey is a tiny box, which holds the greatest lost someday of all—a photo of my bride wearing a white dress, radiant with a promised happily-ever-after, standing next to a man with a face that looks like mine, only younger. I barely recognize that face anymore. He is gone.

The loss of this dream is compounded with a loss I was not expecting—the loss of my tiny cocoon apartment.

Even though I am grateful to be moving to a place where I no longer have to duck the ceiling and doorframes or embody the irony of a motivational speaker living in a basement apartment, I still feel loss. *I feel loss for my sacred meditation corner, where I had gone on many journeys, seeing many new places and finding love from within. Loss for my office space where I wrote my TEDx talk. Loss for my sofa where Simon and I played Lego Jurassic World. Loss for my quiet cul-de-sac of elderly neighbors where Simon and I would practice his T-ball.* I feel loss for those possessions I wish I could take with me but cannot—for anything that can be taken from me is not truly mine. I can only take those memories, which cannot be boxed, donated, or sold.

> ## Grudges keep us stuck. And if we can't move, we can't adapt. We will lose the game.

I begin to weep, mourning this now empty basement apartment where I worked through so much grief. Even though I am getting what I asked for—my desire to speak and travel the world, a new book, a new home—the loss of once again transitioning, downsizing, trimming off more excess that does not serve me, is painful. It hurts. Shedding skin hurts. Yet it is possible, as I see with clarity, to feel both gratitude and sorrow in the same moment: dark and light. As I weep, more and more of it is in gratitude for the bright future ahead and for the haven and home this basement apartment has been for me and Simon.

I am haunted by the whisper: *Was it ever really my home?* Or just another hotel room in my journeys around the world? And in all those temporary abodes I recall, I see so many dreams that were left behind like a sock under the bed. Dreams that no longer serve me in my highest good.

Clarity always comes with a cost.

That cost is usually a dream—a dream that you finally realize no longer belongs on your path, that no longer serves you. A dream that like all those someday boxes cannot come with you. Yet because I am human, I give myself permission to grieve the loss. At the same time, I bow with gratitude for the clarity I've received: clarity that with less of my own agenda, less of my ego stories getting in the way, I am able to see that my journey is not about me or for me, but rather about the greater good and how I might best allow it to work *through* me, as I channel grace, kindness, and compassion to a world that needs more of it. I acknowledge the ultimate act of surrender, which is not a quid pro quo, but a trust that comes with letting go. I know, deep in my bones, that with clarity and with less clutter, stories, and somedays distracting me, I am better equipped now to be a true servant—a spiritual gladiator.

A New Alpha.

And the only place I could have learned this was in my tiny cocoon of a basement apartment, where I would learn to surrender my pictures of You.

Where you stood against the Kyoto sun,
Supernovas and blackholes becoming one,
Linear time folding within fractal time,
Where for a moment, you were never mine,
Only a beautiful mirror.

Thank you.

And may someday I be brave enough to say it to you, face to face, heart to heart.

Ask Yourself

» What is one of your first experiences of being forced or asked to forgive someone? Was it your parent teaching you to accept an apology?

» In your cultural norm, was forgiveness taught more as a commandment and obligation, or was it presented as a self-empowerment modality?

» For you, is taking the "high road" style of forgiveness a superiority, or a true empowering forgiveness? Forgiveness and finding gratitude within require work. It is a discipline, not a flimsy platitude where you simply utter words like, "I forgive them—their karma is their own karma." That is not feeling and working to find the lesson for you in all of your experiences.

» Is your default to be more self-absorbed when something you perceive as bad happens to you, or is it to be self-aware?

» If it is to be self-absorbed, do you understand self-absorption is not necessarily a natural trait but more of a discipline and habit of mind-set that can be honed to be more self-aware and not self-absorbed?

» When you think of forgiveness, do you think you are absolving another person of accountability and of their wrongs?

» Can you see, if positioned so, how forgiveness is empowerment, helping you learn more about who you are, while still holding others accountable with unconditional love?

» What is one experience you don't think you could ever find gratitude for?

» Is it because you cannot or choose not to find gratitude?

Do the Work

Recite these words:

> *Thank you.*
> *I am sorry.*
> *Please forgive me.*
> *I forgive you.*
> *I love you.*

This is the Hawaiian Ho'oponopono prayer of reconciliation and forgiveness. I have said this prayer more times than I could possibly want to in my life. It will benefit you to do the same for those who have wronged you—because you are strong enough. That is the way of the New Alpha male.

In this moment, you will picture whoever frustrates, angers, or hurts you the most. You will see them clearly in your mind's eye and then you will say, "Thank you, I am sorry, please forgive me, I forgive you, I love you," as acrid as the taste in your mouth may be.

Do it again.

And again.

And again.

To progress faster, do it while moving your body. Running or at least walking, recite this prayer while in motion. This will allow the energy to flow two ways—through spoken word and physical exertion—making it doubly powerful.

Do this for you, as growth cannot happen while bitterness still plagues you. Grudges keep us stuck. And if we can't move, we can't adapt. We will lose the game. More importantly, we will lose our freedom and chance at happiness. We were made to let go.

Do the Work

I'm including two "Do the Work" assignments in this chapter because balancing dark and light is one of the most important practices I have to share.

» Begin by holding both palms out and open.

» In one palm hold the hurt from a trauma or wrong committed against you. Rest in that pain and allow it to be. Feel it and breathe through it.

» In the other palm, hold gratitude for the lesson that pain is teaching from the perspective of the greater whole, from a higher consciousness. Acknowledge how much wisdom, growth, and self-awareness you are gaining through this experience.

» Bring both palms together at your heart, allowing yourself to hold the pain and gratitude together.

» Feel it all—really feel it—the anger and gratitude, finding the grace and beauty of our humanity in the union, not in the minimizing polarities.

When I assigned this practice at a workshop, one of my clients bravely stepped up and right off the bat said, "In this hand, I hold pain and anger for my body not being able to bear children." Following her admission of pain, sorrow, and anger she looked at her other hand and said, "In this hand I hold gratitude that motherhood is not biological. That I can love my adopted daughter more deeply than anyone I have ever loved." She brought both hands to her heart center and allowed herself to feel the whole of life, no longer denying either feeling by believing we have to live in a polarized world. She found the beautiful in the whole and fully realized it in her heart.

In the Zone

» Start this one on your knees, with your posture erect, not sitting on your heels.

» Begin with heart drumming.

» Once you have found presence and centeredness, move into Child's Pose, where you will be on your knees, butt resting on your heels. You will lean forward and stretch your hands as far in front of you as you can, bringing your head down to the ground, while keeping your butt still resting on your heels.

» Breathe slowly for a minute, and then focus on one person or one experience you are holding great anger toward. Maybe you have spoken about it to others, maybe you haven't.

» Address the first face to pop into your mind.

» Take ten deep breaths while recalling the person or event.

» Feel your rage and anger and disappointment. You will feel the emotions you need to feel.

» And when the rage has peaked, say, "Thank you."

» And you will hate it.

» But you will say, "Thank you" again.

» And again. As many times as you need to. (It once took me over thirty minutes of saying thank you.)

» And then say, "I'm sorry." Say it again and again.

» And then say, "Please forgive me. I forgive you."

» And once that energy has moved, close with, "I love you." And say thank you again, one more time, and this last time, mean it. Remain in silence in Child's Pose. Don't even focus on breathing. Say thank you as many times as you need to. You will know when you are done. Focus on the peace.

» Only the truly brave can perform this practice. Only the New Alpha is capable of such a task.

There is no time limit to this one. You will know when it is time to stop, as saying thank you will release all the anger, and in place of the rage will be a small feeling of gratitude, as the lesson will begin to appear. In that void of silence, you will see the role you played as well, and the role the other person played for your highest good, reaching toward this moment of clarity.

RECAP

Forgiveness in most cultural norms is a nicety, to get people to get along and let the rest of the community have peace. "Be the bigger person" is a merit badge many of us love to wear in martyrdom, but it still allows people the mind-set to be self-absorbed, not having to really do any reflective work and internal growth.

Forgiveness is not for the weak who are too scared to stand up for themselves. Rather, it is for those who are bravest to look inward and alchemize the pain and projections from others, to learn more about who they truly are beyond the roles and culture they come from. Gratitude and forgiveness are the highest vibrational frequencies we can operate under as human beings. When we take the time to find one person to forgive each day, and send them gratitude, we will find more people giving us more reasons to have gratitude in this life. And gratitude, true empowerment, is the gift that keeps on giving.

10

GAME RECAP

THE SEVEN PRINCIPLES OF PERSEVERANCE are not trophies, nor are they plaques or certificates to put up on a wall. They are not destinations, as there is no arriving with them. They are processes, daily habits. While I speak of them, I do not claim to have perfected them. I do not claim to have mastered them. There are days I fall short in living the Seven Principles of Perseverance, when I am reminded to get back into the gym and practice my bank shots, so to speak.

I didn't just make ten bank shots in a row one day, say "I got this," and never practice my bank shots again. No. It was a daily discipline of testing and honing my skills. Same goes for these principles—making sure we are not functioning in hubris by allowing ourselves to believe we never have to improve or refine them.

While my career will expand and further lessons and keynotes will emerge, I will always refer back to the Seven Principles of Perseverance, because every time I speak about them, I am only reminding myself as well. The Seven Principles of Perseverance are a daily commitment, a consistent choice and challenge to go inward in reflection, unafraid of whatever darkness you may find. In that darkness, you observe the contrast of your light, seeing and accepting your authentic self.

1. Accountability
2. Integrity
3. Compassion
4. Discomfort
5. Acceptance
6. Transformation
7. Forgiveness and Gratitude

Within these Seven Principles of Perseverance is the ability to adapt, not so much necessarily in pursuit of our dreams, but rather in spite of them, as they continually collapse around you. Dreams that you thought would give you clarity and self-worth. While the mirrors shatter around you as you walk this world, heartbreak, perseverance, and a little grit are what take you to clarity, not the accomplishment of dreams themselves like you originally believed. This internal reflection of clarity is more fulfilling than what some distorted reflection on a trophy could ever provide.

As I close, I ask you to promise me, and more importantly, promise yourself, that every time you get knocked down—and you will get knocked down, because that is life—you will get back up one more time. Every single time—*because you choose to*. Promise you will transform those setbacks and heartbreaks into lessons, calling forth the teacher archetype within all of us, because the world needs more teachers and fewer victims. Promise, as you work through the pain and loss that is a part of everyday life, that you will not go inward and shield your heart in bitterness and fear but will be brave enough to rip off the scar tissue, remove your masks, and face forward, allowing your spirit to grow even bigger and stronger, shining so bright that it blinds the world. Promise me you will be gritty enough to love others unconditionally, and more importantly, love yourself unconditionally.

This is winning.

This is Alpha.

A GLADIATOR'S BLESSING

In trust, I have shared parts of me that I have been asked to share, which I can only hope helps others find their own authentic path.

May accountability guide you as you step onto that path with integrity, trusting that as you integrate all aspects of who you are, the right people will integrate with you.

May you always be bold in that journey, accountable for all that happens to you, for you, and through you.

May you always leave the door open with acceptance and with humility for new information and knowledge to expand your horizons into wonder.

May you always embrace and work with discomfort, understanding that it is where the magic happens, knowing we were not born to be caged within our comfort zones.

May you always walk in beauty as you see all the mirrors and illusions around you, knowing they are only reflecting back to you the clarity that your worth is not attached to an outcome.

May you always courageously stare into those mirrors, as you challenge the ill of the world—which is fear.

May you dare to peel away the avatar mask you have been asked to wear that hides your true self, trusting that the world has plenty of room for your quirkiness.

May you hold compassion, not superiority, over those who are still walking their path, knowing it might not even be in this dimension that they discover their eternal worth, as you love them anyway.

May you always treat others with dignity, while holding firm in your compassionate boundaries.

May you always give yourself that same compassion, knowing you are human and that there are days you will struggle, but in that struggle, you will continually rise and your appreciation for your clarity will only grow.

May you be not only more mindful but more heartful as you dance between the dark and the light, knowing that a broken heart is the most valuable thing you can possess in the world, for that is where clarity shines through.

May you be brave enough to walk the path of the heart, understanding that your heart is the gateway to the worlds beyond.

May you always remember that your humanity is your divinity. And may you have the humility to see just how insignificant you truly are, which allows you to see just how beautifully important you are in the greater whole of Creation.

May you embrace the many deaths in this life, of loved ones and dreams, which have and will come your way, but also the many deaths of the person you once were and who you had hoped or believed you had to be.

May you always know that while your culture, values, and idiosyncrasies will die along with your body, you yourself, the star-seed that you are, are eternal, for energy cannot be destroyed, only transmuted and transformed.

And may you find your true self in the ashes. And may the phoenix rise. And may Arcturus shine bright in your sphere.

May the Valkyries of the Halls of Valhalla descend upon you with each death, from each battle well-fought, and carry you next to the battleground of incarnation, where you will always shine because you choose to.

May you always remember the most sacred duty you carry: the duty to love unconditionally.

May your fearless, broken Heyoka heart ride out through these starlit planes of time, blazing a glorious trail beyond the dark and light, as you take your place among the bravest of all: the ones who love unconditionally—so fiercely, so freely, that it burns through the cosmos.

May you meet me in the field, within those fractal echoes, where time has no name, where wonder returns, and where love is eternal.

And may you be bold—*oh, may you always be bold*—in letting your heart guide the way.

ACKNOWLEDGMENTS

There are many mentors who have helped me on this journey, and I would never have been able to find myself in a space to share this book were it not for them:

> To my greatest hero, Hin-mah-too-yah-lat-kekt, "Thunder Rolling Down the Mountain," or your English name: Chief Joseph. Thank you for guiding me on my path around the world, to follow in your footsteps of the peaceful warrior. I can only hope I have adequately honored you in some way.

> Chief Walking Bear, Shaggy Llama, and the rest of my sundance family, thank you for showing me what it means to forgive.

> Strong Eagle, thank you for walking the lonely path before me and showing me how to walk it in beauty.

> Denise Lynch, thank you for always being there for me at the right moment, and also for holding space for me when I needed to grow on my own.

> Christy Foster, thank you for walking this journey with me from our shared backgrounds, showing me through action that the best teachers are first and foremost the greatest students who never stop learning.

> Jan Hull, thank you for showing me wonder and magic again, and for challenging me to truly step into my own and trust my heart.

> Anita Whitworth, thank you for sharing your space with me on those sacred waters.

Robert Ohotto, thank you for showing me I can be woo-woo and a badass at the same time.

Sandra Ingerman, thank you for helping me finally see who and what I truly am, not just in this dimension, but in the many beyond.

Jennifer Brown, thank you for hearing my voice in the crowd and welcoming me to the Sounds True family.

Alice Peck, thank you for brilliantly honing and empowering my true authentic voice to come forward through your editing.

Thank you to all five of you brilliant conduits of the Great Spirit, who have mentored me from afar:

Norman Maclean, in showing me at an early age how to express myself through the written word.

Caroline Myss, in *Sacred Contracts* and your beautiful introduction of the Archetypes of our Psyches.

John Gottman, in your brilliant work on the Four Horsemen of Relationships.

Robert Glover, in your groundbreaking yet powerfully simple exposing of the nice guy in *No More Mr. Nice Guy*.

Wayne Dyer, in the many lonely nights in hotel rooms around the world that your books helped get me through.

Last to my parents, Vance and Tana, thank you for helping me raise Simon and for helping me rise from the ashes during the darkest time of my life.

ABOUT THE AUTHOR

Lance Allred is an international inspirational speaker, trainer, and coach, who has done leadership development for the FBI, Costco, Coldwell Banker, and many others. His TEDx talk, "What Is Your Polygamy?," has been viewed more than 4 million times. His work into avatar decoding has led to him traveling the country as a corporate astrologist.

Lance, with his son, Simon, divides his time between Salt Lake City, Utah, and the Bitterroot Valley of Montana, where he runs various themed retreats. Through his nonprofit organization, Courage and Grit, Lance travels the United States and Canada running basketball camps that focus on emotional quotient (EQ) development for First Nation and deaf teens.

Winner of karaoke night in the Canary Islands, Lance is a recovering cheat at Monopoly who never passes up a good board game night or *One Tree Hill* marathon with his friends.

Learn more at LanceAllred41.com.

ABOUT SOUNDS TRUE

Sounds True is a multimedia publisher whose mission is to inspire and support personal transformation and spiritual awakening. Founded in 1985 and located in Boulder, Colorado, we work with many of the leading spiritual teachers, thinkers, healers, and visionary artists of our time. We strive with every title to preserve the essential "living wisdom" of the author or artist. It is our goal to create products that not only provide information to a reader or listener but also embody the quality of a wisdom transmission.

For those seeking genuine transformation, Sounds True is your trusted partner. At SoundsTrue.com you will find a wealth of free resources to support your journey, including exclusive weekly audio interviews, free downloads, interactive learning tools, and other special savings on all our titles.

To learn more, please visit SoundsTrue.com/freegifts or call us toll-free at 800.333.9185.

sounds true
BOULDER, COLORADO

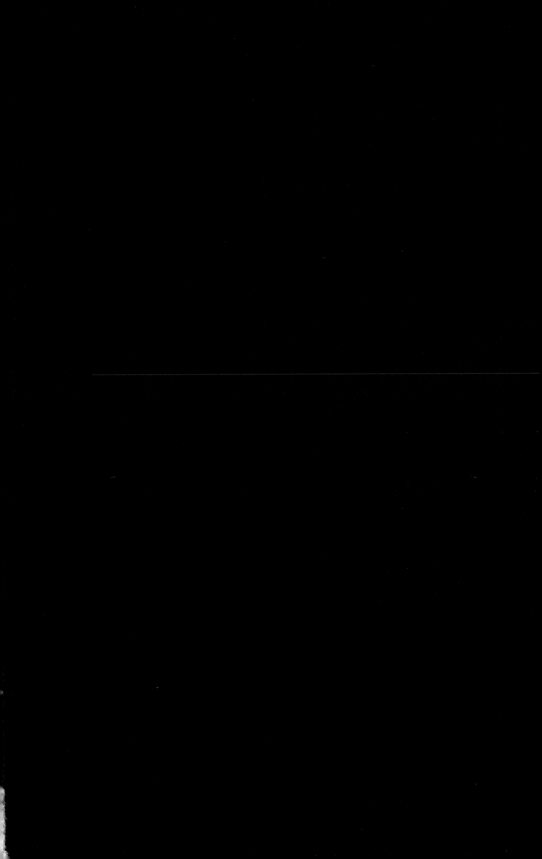